PRAISE FOR NEW BEGINNINGS

"*New Beginnings offers readers a real template for change. Sandy Newbigging writes as he speaks, from the Heart.*"
URSULA JAMES, best-selling author of *The Source*

"*Sandy Newbigging is a very smart guy with a wide open heart whose passion for life is infectious, so it is no surprise that this book is packed with life-changing wisdom.*"
TIMOTHY FREKE, best-selling author of *The Mystery Experience*

"*Just reading this book will lend you enough of a thermal to get you air-borne.*"
BAREFOOT DOCTOR, best-selling author of *Manifesto*

"*If you embrace the tools and wisdom within this book, you will make transformational changes by transcending your inner and outer worlds in a profound way that is rarely taught.*"
JOSEPH CLOUGH, hypnotherapist and author of *Be Your Potential*

"*New Beginnings takes you on a delightful journey to restore peace and happiness to your heart and mind.*"
NICK WILLIAMS, best-selling author of *The Work You Were Born To Do*

"*This is a fabulous book! Sandy mixes punchy tips with ancient wisdom to offer a powerful guide for daily living.*"
SHAMESH ALADINA, best-selling author of *Mindfulness for Dummies*

"*New Beginnings presents deep-rooted spiritual teachings in an easy-to-understand and accessible way. As such it is a rare creation.*"
RICHARD ABBOT, best-selling author of *Natural Living Conferences*

Other Books By Sandy C. Newbigging

Heal the Hidden Cause
Using the 5-Step Mind Detox Method

Life Detox
Clear Physical and Emotional Toxins
from Your Body and Your Life

Life-Changing Weight Loss
3 Steps to Get the Body and Life You Want

Thunk!
How to Think Less for Serenity and Success

NEW BEGINNINGS

TEN TEACHINGS FOR MAKING THE REST OF YOUR LIFE THE BEST OF YOUR LIFE

SANDY C. NEWBIGGING

FINDHORN PRESS

DISCLAIMER

The medical information and all procedures mentioned and contained in this book are not intended to be used or construed as a substitute for professional medical care and advice provided by a physician. People who read this book and make decisions regarding their health or medical care which they believe are based on ideas contained in this book do so at their own risk. The author or publishers are making no medical claims. The author and publishers are not responsible for any adverse effects or consequences resulting from the use of any of the suggestions or information contained in this book, but offer this material as information which the public has a right to hear and utilize at its own discretion.

To Wee Yin

Revised edition published 2013 by Findhorn Press, Scotland
Second edition published 2012 by Thread of Souls Publishing
First edition published 2005 by New Beginnings Publishing

ISBN 978-1-84409-615-2

A CIP record for this title is available from the British Library.

Edited by Jacqui Lewis
Cover design by Sandy Newbigging and Richard Crookes
Interior design by Damian Keenan
Printed and bound in the EU

Published by
Findhorn Press
117-121 High Street,
Forres IV36 1AB,
Scotland, UK

t +44 (0)1309 690582
f +44 (0)131 777 2711
e info@findhornpress.com
www.findhornpress.com

Contents

Let this moment be a new beginning.

The New Edition

• • • •

BY SANDY C. NEWBIGGING

*(and yes, that has been my
surname since birth!)*

"NEWBIGGING, IS THAT YOUR REAL NAME?"... Is one of *the* most popular questions that I've been asked since publishing the first edition of *New Beginnings*. An obvious choice of book title for my first book, you may think. But funnily enough, I didn't actually know what to call this book when I first wrote it. In the end I needed the guidance of a good friend to help me to see a solution that had been staring me in the face the entire time.

Similarly, it is easy to become so distracted by the finer details of the daily routine that we end up missing the bigger-picture point of being alive. By getting caught up with our never-ending list of things to do, we can forget to stop occasionally to 'just be' and enjoy the journey as we move towards creating the life we ultimately want. With this in mind, it is my hope that *New Beginnings* will give you a fresh perspective on the purpose of life – that inspires you to *make every moment matter*. By letting this moment be a new beginning, this book shows you how to embrace the new, let go of problems, attract what you want and, best of all, live happily ever after – not in a land far far away, but in the real-world reality of the here and now.

Since Publishing *New Beginnings*

In the spirit of walking my talk, I set myself the challenge of applying the messages from *New Beginnings* to my own life, with miraculous results.

Soon after the book was originally self-published in 2005 I got invited to work as a therapist on three separate television series that were shown in thirty countries around the world. The publicity from these shows led to me being offered big book deals from major publishing houses (leading to the publication of two best-selling books), run holistic health retreats in the UK, Spain, France, Turkey, Thailand and Australia, and train people from fifteen countries in the Mind Detox Method: a form of therapy that I accidentally created along the way!

Personally, I've made fantastic friendships, visited and lived in beautiful places, become debt-free and even bought myself a convertible *and* a motorbike! All without much stress or struggle, and instead, by focusing on being, loving, and attracting. Exciting, I'm sure you will agree – especially because the latter focus was the *new way of living* that I offered readers in the first edition of *New Beginnings*.

When the Student Is Ready

Perhaps one of the more unexpected developments since writing the first edition of *New Beginnings* was meeting my spiritual teacher and becoming what can best be described as a "modern-day monk". I've meditated for thousands of hours since, had the opportunity to teach meditation around the world and published another book on the subject – *Thunk!* (Findhorn Press, 2012).

When you combine the experience that has come from working with a wide variety of people at my clinics, courses, and retreats, guidance from my spiritual teacher and insight gained from countless hours of meditation, my experience of life has moved on somewhat since I wrote *New Beginnings* in 2005. Now feels like the perfect time to offer a new edition of this much-loved book.

Ten Inner Teachings

Being present and developing an enlightened perspective on life circumstances is wisdom that never goes out of fashion and is by its very nature timeless. Fans of the first edition of *New Beginnings* will notice that the structure and tagline of this book have changed significantly.

When writing this edition, ten stand-alone and significant "teachings" revealed themselves to me through my writing. Furthermore, having lived these teachings over the past few years I know they can have a dramatic impact on a person's life. So in an attempt to communicate the importance of knowing and living these teachings, I felt that only a grand tagline involving the statement *"Making the Rest of Your Life the Best of Your Life"* would do. But the changes to this edition don't stop there, mainly due to a shift in priorities that I've made over the past few years.

From Knowing to Being

In 2005, I was starting out as a writer. Being the new kid on the block I felt I had to prove myself and wanted to become known as a good teacher. However now, in 2013, I am far more interested in *being the teaching*. This shift, although it appears simple on the surface, is profound, and by far the biggest and most important shift in priorities I have ever made. I have discovered that it is the difference between *knowing about* cool spiritual concepts and *directly experiencing*, in this lifetime, true wealth, happiness, peace of mind and freedom from problems.

By offering a fully updated new edition of *New Beginnings* I want to give more guidance on how to make the shift between *knowing about* what you want and *experiencing it* in the real world. The difference is worth everything. There are plenty of conceptually enlightened people on Earth; however, what this planet needs most right now is people living enlightened lives.

Here's to you living it!

Sandy C. Newbigging
May 2013

I Dare You!

. . . .

BY DAVID R. HAMILTON PHD

THERE IS LITTLE DOUBT THAT THE QUALITY OF OUR INTENTIONS AFFECTS THE QUALITY OF OUR LIVES. Even scientists, over the last few years, have proven unequivocally that our thoughts affect our bodies – our brain, heart, immune system and even our genes. But our intentions also affect everything around us; the quality of our intentions affects the quality of our life circumstances.

It is the place within us that these intentions come from that is important. Intentions rooted in love and appreciation are proven to bring about positive changes – both to a person's health and to their life circumstances.

In fact, scientific studies have shown that feeling genuine appreciation for a person boosts your own immune system, protecting you from harmful microforms. In a real sense, too, appreciation of your gift of life boosts your immunity to life's microforms, i.e. "negative" life circumstances.

Although, as this book explains, there are no negative circumstances really, only circumstances that we label as negative. It is only our way of looking at things that labels them as either positive or negative and once we label them, our judgements about them affect how we feel.

So the power to feel good is within us, right now. It's down to how we choose to look at things. As Sandy says: "*It is not what happens, but instead, the meaning you attach to what happens that determines whether you experience a 'joy-full' or 'problem-full' life."*

Scientific studies show this quite clearly. Say a person is running late for an appointment. The mental and emotional stress of their lateness causes biochemical changes in their body – elevates stress hormone levels, speeds up the aging process and even changes their genes. But it's not being late itself, but rather the thoughts *about* being late, that cause these biochemical changes. Simply being late is a neutral external event that does nothing to the body or to life. But the inner meaning attached to it does.

So, for our own sake, we need to learn how to accept and flow with life circumstances. This way we don't label things as negative and so don't introduce ourselves to stress; instead, we introduce ourselves to joy. One of the best ways to do this is, as Sandy encourages, stop dwelling on the past, stop worrying about the future, stop waiting until things are different, better or improved, and instead embrace the newness of now to feel joyful.

So, go on. Apply Sandy's Ten Inner Teachings to your daily life and see what happens. I dare you!

"If You Always Do What
You've Always Done,
You Will Always Get
What You've Always Got."

MARK TWAIN

Freedom to Choose

• • • •

ANCIENT WISDOM FOR
LIBERATED LIVING

EVERY SECOND OF EVERY DAY OFFERS A NEW BEGINNING. Right now, the forces of creation are miraculously and magnificently coming together to give birth to a brand new moment bursting with potential and possibilities. What you do with it is ultimately your choice, which is what the Ten Inner Teachings are all about. Used individually or collectively, they give you the freedom to choose between peace or pain, confusion or clarity, problems or perfection, procrastination or action and failure or success.

Reading the teachings, you will see if you have, out of habit and conditioning, been playing the victim, dwelling on the past, complaining about the present or letting fear about the future limit your life today. Applying the teachings, you will awaken the ability within you to consciously choose to celebrate your gift of life, melt into the magnificent moment and boldly and brilliantly use all that happens to evolve, for the benefit of yourself and all of humanity.

New Beginnings offers a new way of liberated living – one free from problems and bursting with blessings.

Each moment you have a life-affirming choice to make. You can habitually judge and resist what happens and in the process create unnecessary stress, pain, and suffering for yourself. Or, you can choose to accept life and let the universe guide and help you. You attach meaning to every event that happens. As a result, it is not what happens, but instead, the meaning you attach to what happens that determines whether you experience a "joy-full" or "problem-full" life. This book is about letting go of perceiving problems as problems – for good!

When it comes to getting your goals, you can either achieve what you want with stress and struggle, or you can attract what you want with effortless ease and the whole universe on your side. With this book I will show you how to become a magnet for miracles with the power of positive focus, uplifting emotions, presence, praise and non-attachment. Within these pages are powerful strategies for inviting more of what you want into your life.

Inner Teachings for Transforming Your External World

"Be the change you want to see in the world," as said by Mahatma Gandhi, is to this day a very widely known and used quote. These ten words have had such a great impact on humanity because without changing yourself, you have very little chance of having any lasting impact on the world.

> *Building the body and life you want requires the right INNER foundation.*

When embarking on making improvements it is vital that you embrace the evolutionary inner work that is usually required. To guide you, *New Beginnings* shares ten inner teachings for making the rest of your life the best of your life. By focusing on cultivating a more positive and productive inner relationship with life, you create a powerful platform for making genuine and long-lasting changes to your external life circumstances. Not only that, but you also get to experience 200% of life!

Is There More to Life Than This?

In my opinion, evolution is one of our primary purposes in life. By evolution, I'm not referring to becoming less hairy and standing more upright, but instead to raising our level of consciousness. As human beings, our most natural way of being is to embrace the new, live free from problems, attract what we want and be joyful. Most people experience feeling joy by being completely in the moment, letting go of problems by looking at things differently, and by experiencing meaningful coincidences that help them to attract what they want.

Quite often, however, we do this unconsciously, without noticing; just appreciating and enjoying what's really going on. As we raise our level of consciousness, we become more *inwardly* aware, peaceful and present. We live less in the past and future and more in the divine presence that exists within the magnificent moment. We simultaneously become more purposeful, passionate and impactful in our *external* actions too. Choosing how we want to respond to life, we become more aware of what's really going on within the universe as a whole. In turn, we get to enjoy 200% of life – living fully both inwardly and externally – in an enlightened way.

The Purpose of Life Is to Live

Ever wondered what the meaning of life is? You are not alone. It is a universal question that millions of people have considered at least at some point. Unfortunately, many get stuck finding an answer, due to both the magnitude of the question and the fact that they mistakenly think their purpose relates to what they do. In fact, I know people in their sixties and seventies who are *still* trying to figure out their purpose. Feeling less-than, lost and confused as to what they are supposed to be *doing* with their life. All the while, missing their life as the years tick by!

You too could spend years trying to discover it; waiting for your eureka moment – when it all becomes clear and you finally discover *the meaning of life*. Or you can opt to keep the answer simple (as the truth always is) and consider the liberating possibility that the *purpose of life is to live*. Does this sound like a rather simplistic purpose of life? Were you hoping for something a bit more deep and meaningful? Sorry to let you down! But please bear with me. If you apply this simple truth to your life, I promise that you will rediscover magic.

Are You Surviving or Thriving?

How many people do you know who are living fully? By this I mean experiencing 200% of life. *Inwardly* fully knowing and experiencing the depth and magnitude of Who They Are (see Chapter 4) and *externally* fully embracing every moment with absolute passion, fearlessness, unconditional joy and limitless love.

Personally, for most of my life I didn't know what it was to live fully. Then one day I came across a quote by a spiritual teacher called MSI, which said:

"Life is meant to be lived in eternal joy, infinite freedom, unconditional love and unbounded awareness. Any other life is utterly missing the point of being born a human."

Wow! These words both scared my socks off and simultaneously made me feel as excited as a kid in a candy store. For the first time in my life I had been given a peek at the kind of human experience that was possible for me during *my* lifetime. As I reread the statement a few more times it also became crystal-clear to me that I hadn't been living fully. At best I'd been getting by. Surviving, not thriving. Governed by fear, focused on trying to avoid things I didn't want and aiming to get to my deathbed with as safe and comfortable a ride as possible.

"Life should not be a journey to the grave
with the intention of arriving safely
in an attractive and well preserved body,
but rather a skid in sideways,
champagne in one hand, strawberries in the other,
thoroughly used up, totally worn out
screaming woo-hoo what a ride!"

GEORGE CARLIN

Now I'm passionate about living. Really living! Squeezing every bit of life out of each moment. By exploring what it means to live in eternal joy, unconditional love and unbounded awareness I've discovered that my purpose is less about what I do and much more about experiencing *who I am as I do*. What I'm doing has become secondary to noticing, appreciating and enjoying the miracle of life itself. More and more I see that the purpose of life is to live by learning how to love, playing fully in the world and experiencing maximum enjoyment at every moment.

ABOUT THIS BOOK

As you read the **TEN INNER TEACHINGS** you may notice that they cover three distinct areas:

Embracing the new
Letting go of problems
Manifesting miracles

They are structured this way for a good reason. Attracting miracles may involve certain aspects of your life changing. However, I have found that if you focus on changing life without first being present and loving yourself, then your intentions for making changes can be fear-based. Negative intention can cause long-term problems because a) there is a focus on what you *don't* want and b) you make yourself a victim to the weather of your life circumstances, i.e. how "good" or "bad" your career, relationships or finances happen to be.

Become a Magnet for Miracles!

On the other hand, when you embrace the new and let go of problems, you learn how to be present and align your attention with the power of the universe. From being in the here and now, your positive intentions become much more powerful and you become a magnet for miracles. Every day becomes a celebration of your evolution, an opportunity to live with passion, purpose and love – for the benefit of yourself and all of humanity.

Living from love benefits everything in the cosmos.

"The Reason That We Know Everything Is Perfect Is Because It Is Happening."

ECKHART TOLLE

PART ONE

The Ten Inner Teachings

• • • •

**FOR MAKING THE REST OF YOUR LIFE
THE BEST OF YOUR LIFE**

CHAPTER ONE

Outer Reflects Inner

· · · ·

INNER TEACHING ONE

You Get What You Project,
So Start By Cleaning Up Your Self-Image

ORANGE TREES DON'T GROW PEACHES. Obvious statement to make, perhaps, but it serves to start your new beginning by shining an illuminating light on one of the foremost of the natural laws that govern this universe: namely, that you reap what you sow.

External Life Echoes Your Inner Expectations

Inner thoughts, including your beliefs, intentions and expectations, are the inner seeds of your external life circumstances. Meaning that your self-image, including your personal opinions about who you think you are and what you believe you are capable of, shapes your external health, wealth, relationships, living and working environments, and so on.

The seeds that you sow become the life that you grow.

Do You Need to Clean Up Your Self-Image?

Intentionally directing the universe in ways that will create more of the things you want (I say "intentionally" because you are already directing the direction of your universe!) begins with making sure your inner self-image reflects the outer new things that you wish to bring into your life. Or in other words, that you know in your heart and mind that you are worthy of receiving what it is you want.

Even if you don't immediately believe it to be true, if you start to intentionally think about yourself as a more positive, passionate, confident, adventurous and abundant person, you will begin to make decisions that will create a person and life that reflects your self-image. On the other hand, the same is also true if you perceive yourself as a dull, timid, failure who lives a poor, boring and loveless life. If you go on thinking negative things about yourself, then you will not deem yourself deserving of allowing miracles to flow through your life.

If you aren't seeing what you want in your life, then it's time to clean up your self-image.

Ultimately it can be your choice to shape your self-image in a way that will help you to feel worthy of miracles. Let now be the time you choose to take control of the opinions you have about yourself. The first step is to become aware of how you have been thinking up until today.

To do this, use the "Your Self-Image" and "Sources of Self-Speak" Tools on pages 115 and 116 in Appendix 1. From there I suggest you then explore the possibility that you might *already* be much more amazing than you think you are with the "My Achievements" Tool on page 117. After which point you will be ready to progress to one of my favourite Tools ever – a "Personal Power Statement" (on pages 118-119 – for creating a life-saving affirmation that you can think often to train your brain to automatically be more positively loving towards yourself.

A Personal Power Statement Saved My Life!

I first wrote a Personal Power Statement when I was twenty-three years old. I was stuck in a dead-end job, lacked passion and felt that my young age was a barrier to working in this field. To turn my thinking around my Personal Power Statement was: *"I'm a fired-up achiever with youth on my side!"* (Cheesy perhaps, but it was the exact opposite to how I actually perceived myself at the time so it was the perfect Personal Power Statement for me). I wrote it on a piece of folded card and sat it on my desk at work. People would occasionally come by and smirk at my statement; however, keeping it there was a sign of my commitment to making it a reality. To hide it would have completely undermined its power.

Then one Thursday afternoon my Personal Power Statement quite literally saved my life. My contract was due for renewal and after a disappointing meeting with the management team I was informed that they had decided not to give me what I had asked for. They then proceeded to give me until the end of the day to sign the contract or not bother returning to work the next day!

That afternoon, as I held my new contract in my hands I found myself at a choice point. I could take the safe road by signing the contract, thus continuing in a job that didn't make my heart happy. Or I could go it alone without the corporate comfort blanket by leaving to embark on a career in coaching and training (approximately ten years before I thought I was ready!).

Remarkably, as I considered my options, the thought *"I'm a fired-up achiever with youth on my side!"* kept springing to the forefront of my mind. As it did, I felt a confidence building in my belly, along with a sense that my self-worth was rising up too; giving me permission not to settle for second best and to make the kind of decision that *a fired-up achiever with youth on his side* would make.

The rest, as they say, is history. I'm so happy I didn't sell out and my Personal Power Statement gave me the courage to stand up for what I wanted, despite most people around me thinking I was mad to leave.

`TOP TIP` **Shout It from the Rooftops!**

There is great power in declaring your Personal Power Statement to the world. Saying this, I wouldn't suggest you rush to *your* rooftop and start shouting your Personal Power Statement, in case you get arrested or fall off and injure yourself! Instead, I recommend you do it the more modern way – via Facebook and Twitter! When you do, remember to share your post with me so I can see it – www. facebook.com/minddetoxman. I love reading Personal Power Statements because they are such an easy way to clean up your self-image by ...

> *Being kind and gentle towards yourself. Encouraging yourself like a good friend would, and appreciating that you can create yourself anew, starting now.*

You Are Worthy!

Irrespective of what's happened during your life so far, open your mind to the possibility that you are a human being fully worthy of living a deliciously divine destiny.

So much has gone into giving you life and so much continues to work miraculously to keep you alive. Blessed with the gift of life, you have the potential and opportunities to both feel fantastic and manifest a magnificent reality. Believe it or not, as a human being you have been specially designed to enjoy your gift of life. Your most natural way of being is to experience peace, joy and love, without needing specific reasons to do so. You were born free to live a breathtakingly awe-inspiring existence – overflowing with all the things you could possibly want. Imagine that!

If you have disconnected yourself from the reality that you are a free and powerful human being, then now is your invitation and opportunity to open your mind to new ways of perceiving yourself.

The Amazing New You

Amazingly, you are a "new you" every single moment of every day. Today is a new day, and you are a new you. You are different to who you were yesterday. Different to who you were two seconds ago! You may not think you're new; you may feel the same – but that doesn't mean you are *actually* the same. It doesn't matter what you have or haven't done, you are still always becoming something new. If you are alive, you are becoming something new.

Even reading this book is causing changes within your body and mind that are making you different to what you were a few seconds ago. You are new! Embracing the new is about opening your eyes and ears and tuning in to your experience of life. Be aware of the newness that exists in everyone you meet, even if they are family or friends that you've met a thousand times. Be aware of the newness in every place you go, even if you've been there countless times. Look for it. Listen for it. Feel for it.

Be willing to embrace the newness in everything. Choose to wake up to the fresh magnificence of you, other people and the world.

You may not think your mind, body and life experiences are new, but again, that doesn't mean that they are actually the same. If you haven't noticed the newness, it doesn't mean it isn't there, it just means you haven't noticed it! The key to embracing the new is to first be willing to notice newness. This is so important because noticing newness automatically leads to the inner recognition that you have countless opportunities to make positive changes and create your day however you want (more about this in Chapter 3).

Who Do You Want to Be from Now on?

Every day you can decide who you want to be today. You are not fixed in stone. Neither are you a victim to your past. You always have the power to choose. Do you want to notice the beauty in all things? Do you want to have fun and be playful throughout your day? Do you want to feel calm, confident or content? Do you want to really appreciate everyone and everything? Do you want to love things perfectly, instead of trying to find perfect things to love? Explore further how you want to be in the next chapter, by discovering your heart's highest hope...

CHAPTER TWO

Highlight
Highest Hope

. . . .

INNER TEACHING TWO

Save Time And Effort By Not Looking In The Wrong Places

FOR THE UNIVERSE TO BE ABLE TO DELIVER WHAT YOU WANT, YOU MUST FIRST KNOW WHAT YOU WANT! Getting super-clear on what I call your heart's highest hope can be the difference that makes all the difference. To help, I'm giving you an imaginary magic wand and with it you can have any one wish. What would you ask for? Take a moment to consider your options.

If you could have absolutely anything, what would it be?

Knowing your heart's highest hope is one of the most important things you can *ever* know. Highlighting your heart's highest hope by living each day super-clear on what you ultimately want, more than anything else, helps you to stop wasting time, focus on what's useful, make better decisions and massively increase your chances of enjoying it.

You Are Not Alone

Having had the opportunity to ask thousands of people this question, I've been fascinated to observe how, irrespective of health, wealth, nationality or background, there are two answers that keep cropping up.

Almost everyone I've met wants the magic wand to bring happiness or inner peace. (I affectionately refer to what they want as "happeaceness" because, although I always say they can have *one thing*, most people want both!). Other close contenders include love, bliss, confidence, fearlessness, wisdom, contentment and union with God. What would *you* want if anything were possible?

Stop Looking Outside for Inner Experiences

Let me give you a top tip here. If a physical or external thing comes to mind, such as better health, more money or meeting a life partner, ask yourself *Why do I ultimately want it?* Whenever I ask people this, they usually say something like: "If I met someone then I would experience love" or "If I was healthy then I'd be happy." So by that rationale, their highest desire is actually love or happiness. See the difference? More often than not, the heart's greatest desire is a positive *inner* experience.

Any true new beginning requires you to know where you want to end up. So stop reading until you have properly considered what your heart's highest hope is. This book is all about helping you to get it. Knowing it can help you to save massive amounts of time and effort because you naturally stop looking for an *inner experience* outside yourself, and thus reap the immediate benefits.

An Enlightening Dialogue

When my spiritual teacher asked me what I wanted more than

anything else I passionately answered: "PEACE!" However, the next question almost had me fall off my chair. He enquired: "Great, so if you want peace, how much of your day is focused on making that your living experience?"

I had to be honest and admit: "I'm really busy right now, so not that much!"

"OK, so why are you so busy then?" my teacher asked compassionately.

"So that I can get my body, relationships, finances and life how I want them to be so that one day I can relax and…" (I remember pausing as the boulder-sized penny dropped) "… enjoy some PEACE!"

With the help of that enlightening dialogue I saw how I was habitually putting my heart's highest hope on hold; waiting until I fixed, changed and improved my life circumstances. Trying to feel good on the inside by perfecting my life on the outside, I was waiting for a future feeling that never came. Out of reach and dependent on external factors largely out of my direct control. Sound familiar?

> *Have you been working hard to get to the mythological place called "there"?*
> *What if "there" is "here"? It has been all the time.*

Being Peaceful Does Not Make You Passive

Despite your heart's greatest desire being an inner experience, this does not mean that you have to give up on improving your external life circumstances. You are here to enjoy 200% of life after all. By doing this, you are free to fully experience the peace and joy that comes from being present (see Chapters 3 and 4), while making whatever improvements to your life circumstances you want. In reality, I find that when people are resting in their heart's greatest desire by being fully present, they are naturally much more willing to think big about how they'd love their external life to be. It's a genuine win–win!

Dreaming BIG like Little Caterpillars

The first step to creating your dream life is to allow yourself to dream again.

When I look at caterpillars I like to imagine that they dream big and bright about how they'd like their lives to be. I take inspiration from the possibility that they choose to ignore their current set of circumstances and instead focus their attention and efforts on manifesting their dream life. Instead of beating themselves up about what they are to begin with, caterpillars appear to accept themselves in the knowing that they need to start where they are to get to where they want to be. By allowing themselves to dream big about how they want their life, they allow themselves to fulfil their potential by evolving into the beautiful butterflies they were destined to be.

Unfortunately, too few people share the same positive attitude as the little caterpillars. Too many tend to base their future dreams upon their current set of circumstances. They create and accept the illusion that they will never be able to live the life of their dreams and instead settle for what they've got. They disconnect themselves from the reality that they are infinitely powerful human beings able to manifest the reality they desire.

As a Child, You Knew How to Dream
Whenever you were thinking about what you wanted for your birthday or Christmas, you would let your imagination run free.

You focused on what you wanted and all the reasons *why* you wanted it. You would allow yourself to get excited, tell lots of people and focus your attention on getting it.

Many adults stop dreaming because they forget to enjoy the thought of *what* they want, and instead cloud their vision by focusing too much upon *how* they're going to get it. They base their future upon the past and focus on the reasons why they probably won't get what they want. In doing so they quickly talk themselves out of pursuing their dreams. They fail to learn from the little caterpillars by accepting their current set of circumstances and asking "How would I like things to be from now on?"

Living in Accordance with Your Values

When deciding how you want your life circumstances to be, it is highly beneficial to set goals that are in line with the things that you value most. Your values are the things in life that are important to you. Values can either be general-life or context-specific values. As the names suggest, general-life values relate to the things that are important to you in life, whereas context-specific values relate to different areas of your life, such as your career or relationships.

> *By living in accordance with your personal values you will feel more fulfilled.*

General-life values include: love, freedom, security, intimacy, growth, fun, integrity and peace, whereas context-specific values for your relationships might include: understanding, intimacy, humour, similar interests, kindness and encouragement. See pages 121-122 for the "Valuable Life" and "Valuable Hints" Tools to get clear on your values. By discovering and clarifying your values, you can:

- Understand what makes you tick: what's important and what's not
- Recognize what's truly essential in your life
- Create a map that can guide you through decisions in your life
- Forecast in advance whether achieving something will be fulfilling or not.

There is a direct link between values and fulfilment. If you are feeling fulfilled in certain areas of your life, it means that you are meeting your personal values in these areas. If, on the other hand, you are feeling internal tension or conflict, it could be the result of one or more of your personal values being suppressed or challenged. It is therefore extremely useful to be aware of what they are and ensure that you are living your life in accordance with them.

Getting Super-Clear on Your Ideal Life
You are the architect of your life situation. Every day, whether you are aware of it or not, you spend twenty-four hours designing your life. The great news is that it is up to you how you use your time and there are no limits to the incredible day you can build.

Prepare yourself to succeed by having clarity. Doing so will allow you to plan the most appropriate action steps to close the gap between where you are and where you want to be. Please see pages 124-133 for the "Personal Profile", "101 Life Clarity Questions" and "Lifetime Focus" Tools to start to get super-clear on how you want your life situation to be.

Top Tips for Total Clarity
Here are some of my favourite top tips for attaining absolute clarity about your life-situational goals:

`TOP TIP #1` **Get Specific**

Don't know what you want? Dividing your life into the following smaller, more manageable chunks helps massively:

- Love and romance with partner
- Family and friend relationships
- Health and vitality
- Career and work
- Wealth and access to resources
- Living and working environment
- Fun and recreation
- Personal development and growth
- Contribution to others
- Spirituality and self-awakening

For each area, consider how things are now and how you could improve them to enjoy your ultimate life.

`TOP TIP #2` **Do What You Love**

Life is precious so there's no point wasting it doing things you don't love. Most people I meet know what they don't want, but when asked what they *do* want they can quickly become perplexed. The good news is that if you know what you don't like then I'd suggest you already know what you love. You simply need to flip your dislikes to find their opposites. In doing so, you discover what you want. Use the "Love Hate Review" Tool on page 134 to explore this and also the "Feel Good Times" Tool on page 135 to get to know what you truly enjoy.

`TOP TIP #3` **Choose Goals That Are Impactful**

Invest time and energy in attracting goals that will have the greatest positive impact upon your life. To help, I've created a couple of Tools in Appendix 1 including "Impact Goals" and "Scoring Goals" (pages 136 and 137) to help you to pursue goals that are genuinely worth manifesting.

TOP TIP #4 Share Your Dreams with Dreamers

When learning to dream again it is wise to only share your dreams with people who are willing to think BIG too. Otherwise you can be talked out of going for what you want. Surrounding yourself with people who support and encourage you is vital when embarking on a genuine new beginning. Recruit "Your Dream Team" using the Tool on page 138 in Appendix 1.

TOP TIP #5 Make Your Goals M.E.A.N.T. T.O. B.E.

Have the universe on your side when going for your goals by designing them in such a way that makes them feel "meant to be" and inevitable. M.E.A.N.T. T.O. B.E. is an acronym that is explained in more detail on page 139. Following the guidelines provided enables you to ensure your individual goals are congruent with your beliefs. There is also a Tool called "Manifesting M.E.A.N.T. T.O. B.E. Goals" on page 140 that you can use to create a clear and compelling image in your mind of what you want.

Clarity is power.
Without it you can end up living in the dark.

Remember to keep your heart's highest hope as your primary focus when exploring goals to change your external life circumstances. By applying the next Inner Teaching you can discover how it is possible to create your ideal future while also enjoying the journey...

CHAPTER THREE

Be Here Now

. . . .

INNER TEACHING THREE

Plug Into The Universal Point Of Power

**HARNESSING THE POWER OF THE UNIVERSE REQUIRES YOUR AT-
TENTION TO BE ALIGNED WITH THE POINT IN SPACE AND TIME IN
WHICH THE UNIVERSE EXISTS AND OPERATES.** In reality, *everything*
in this universe exists now. Now is all there is. Your life is happening now. In fact, your life is nothing more than the present moment
you're in. Now is all you have. If you are lucky enough to wake up
tomorrow, open your eyes and be blessed with the gift of life, all
you have is one more now!

Embracing each and every new beginning is about embracing
the now. Whenever you are in the now, you are noticing all that is
now. Whenever you are thinking about the past, your focus is out
of the now and you are in your head, thinking. Whenever you are
thinking about the future, your focus is out of the now, and again
you are in your head.

Now is outside your thoughts in the direct and immediate *inner*
experience of this magnificent moment. If you're not enjoying as much
love, beauty, mystery, fun or happiness as you would like, it doesn't
mean these things aren't already present in your life. It just means you

aren't noticing them. By getting out of your head and being in the moment, you will notice that your heart's greatest desire is present.

Get out of your head; get into the now and notice.

Missing the magnificent moment can create an awful amount of unnecessary pain, stress and struggle. You risk spending your life in lack, always wanting more than what you have; you risk never feeling fulfilled. You risk regretting things about your past or pining for times that were "better". If you ever say, *"I'll be happy when ..."* or *"I'll be able to relax when ..."* then you are needlessly postponing your enjoyment of the moment you're in. You are metaphorically taking what you want, more than anything else, and throwing it to a time in the future that will never come.

Why Won't It Ever Come?

Waiting is a thinking pattern that eternally keeps your heart's highest hope out of reach.

You will keep throwing what you want into the future until you stop engaging with that old thinking pattern and notice that you can only ever experience peace, happiness or whatever your heart wants *now*. Life is too precious to postpone enjoying it. Instead, decide what you want and learn how to be attentive enough to notice it within yourself, and eventually within everyone and everything, now. Again, if you don't experience it immediately, it doesn't mean it isn't there, it just means you have not cultivated the skill of noticing it, yet!

Now Is Instantly Forever

Time is useful for making practical arrangements, such as catching buses, making dinner reservations and going to the cinema. Nevertheless, to properly understand embracing the now you need to let go of your concept of time.

Every moment is new and every moment is nothing to do with time. The now is not measurable or linear. It just is. If you were to think of the now within the context of time, then it would be smaller than the shortest instant while being longer than forever. The now is both immediate and infinite, simultaneously. Try to get your head around that! Thankfully you don't have to because being present requires you to leave the mind behind and freefall into the full and immediate inward experience of the here and now. Sound scary? It need not be.

Now Is Both Safe and Serene

It is forever new and fresh and full of vibrant life. When you reconnect with now you discover that it is much more appealing to be here than in any other time. You notice that once something has happened, it is immediately in the past. Gone. Forever, even if it only happened a moment ago. If you start thinking about what happened, you go into your head, leaving behind the amazing possibilities this new moment has to offer. You start missing life.

Going into the past regurgitates the old. The past is dead. Please don't waste a second looking back to some other time because you will not find your heart's greatest desire there. Only here. You see, even if you are successful in your quest to make your past and future perfect, you can only experience your heart's greatest desire now.

You cannot experience your heart's greatest desire in the past or future. You can only experience it now. So why keep looking to some other time for what can only be experienced now?

What's happened in your past or what might happen in your future is irrelevant to whether you can experience peace, love and happiness in this moment. It is impossible for you to directly experience anything truly fulfilling in any time other than now. If you get what I'm saying here it will change your life forever!

Negative Emotions: A Thing of the Past!

Thinking about the past or future opens you up to feeling bad because negative emotions need *time* in order to exist. Fear and anxiety normally involve thinking about potential future scenarios, whereas thinking about the past can create anger, sadness or guilt. Although you experience negative emotions like these in the now, you feel them by thinking about past experiences or imagining potential future scenarios. See the difference? Liberation from negative emotions comes from learning to let go of thinking about other times and focusing on now.

When you are fully present, attentive to now, you naturally feel good.

But don't take my word for it – see the "Peace Exists Now" Tool on page 141 in Appendix 1. If you ever find yourself feeling negative emotions, notice where your attention is. Guaranteed you will either be thinking about the past or future or judging the moment you're in as bad (which, incidentally, is still not being present because you've left the moment to think about how now isn't how you think it should be). If you're feeling negative emotions, you will never be here and now. It's impossible.

Invest time in developing the ability to be aware of the newness that exists within yourself, everyone you meet and every place you go. Look for it, listen for it and feel for it in every moment. As you do, notice how colours become brighter and sounds become clearer. See the "Stop Watch", "Making the Mundane Magical" and "3C Vision" Tools on pages 142-144 to begin practising being here now.

Notice how life becomes a magical adventure to be savoured and enjoyed. Embrace every step of your life journey. Acknowledge that the journey *is* the destination. You have the power within you now to turn things round in an instant.

> *The magnificent moment is nothing to do with getting anywhere. You arrived the day you were born. You are complete as you are now.*

A Clear-Cut Formula

Being present is very clear-cut: you are either *in the moment* or *in your mind* thinking about the past and future. Despite this, many people find it hard, give up on it and rarely experience the wonder and awe of what it is to be fully present, mainly due to a major piece of the present-moment puzzle missing.

Noticing what's happening now is only a part of being present. For you to fully experience the peace, love, joy and contentment that is your birthright to experience now, you must rediscover your Being.

Your Being is the permanent aspect of *you* that is already always present. Read that sentence again! There is an aspect of you that is *already* present. By resting back into your *Being*, you automatically become *present* (hence the well-known phrase *Being Present*). Better still, when you are resting into your Being you can experience life in its perfection, free from problems, and become a magnet to miracles.

SO HOW DO YOU BE? Let's explore this life-changing question in the next chapter ... now!

CHAPTER FOUR

Rest in Being

· · · ·

INNER TEACHING FOUR

You're Already Doing
A Brilliant Job *Being* You

COURAGEOUS CONTENTMENT COMES FROM KNOWING YOU ARE NOT YOUR LIFE CIRCUMSTANCES. You are not your job title, marital status, nationality or any other label you may be able to attach to your identity. You are something much more than you think. You are life.

Confusing your life for what you do is one of the most common causes of problems on the planet. It can make your peace and happiness become victim to your life circumstances, as you *need* them to be a certain way for you to be OK. This leads to living in fear, the need to overly control and manage your life and miss the brilliant glory of what you truly are.

> *Your being is what you are.*
> *Your life circumstances are what you do.*

There is a difference between your *life* and your *life circumstances*. Your life is your Being and your Being is What You Are. (Hence, human **Being**!) Whereas your life circumstances are the collection of things that you do with your life – including your job, relationships and finances. The fact that you are alive proves that you have life. Otherwise you'd be dead! Even more remarkably, it is impossible for your Being ever to become broken, bad or sick. It is always pristine and perfect. Therefore, whether you believe it or not, your *life* is *already* perfect.

Consider this: for how much of your day are you inwardly aware of your own Being? Most people I meet put much more attention on what they are doing. In doing so, they leave very little attention, if any, to be attentive to their Being. But if you stop a moment and just be, you will notice that You are here. Now, that may seem like an obvious thing to say; nevertheless, how often do you appreciate how perfectly You are Being You? Or said another way, how perfectly You are Being Life?

> *Irrespective of life circumstances, you are always being*
> *life perfectly.*

You may have some preconceived ideas about who or what you think you *should* be, but that doesn't stop you Being You perfectly, right now. Embracing the new is about focusing less on doing things to try to improve life circumstances, and instead, making it your moment-to-moment purpose to explore Being Life. As you become increasingly curious about exploring Being Life, your life circumstances have less of an impact upon your peace, love and joy. It is still nice to have a career you find rewarding or meet a great partner. But these external things become less important compared to Being Life, when you see that it is the difference between enlightened living and existing ignorant to the unbounded brilliance of Who You Think You Are. Explore Who You Think You Are using the Tool on page 145.

*To be enlightened is to know and experience
the truth of Who You Are.*

Make It a Priority to Notice Your Being

What aspect of you does not change? You are not what you do because what you do is temporary. It comes and it goes. However, everything that happens during your day does so within the constant context of your Being. Your Being is always present, vast and free from limitations or problems. It is the still silent conscious awareness that is observing this moment happen.

Even now, your Being is present and observing this word being read. To notice it you can let your attention rest inward. Intend to notice this moment happening and you can become aware of the still silent watcher observing from behind your eyes. A presence of Being living within your body. An aliveness existing within peace, irrespective of what's happening in the external world.

Being Is beyond What Happens in Your Life

Living aware of your Being is incredibly liberating. When you are resting aware of your Being you are free from fear because nothing external can impact your inner experience of peace and perfection.

*You no longer have to rely on your life circumstances being
any particular way for you to be contented and happy.*

Freedom is possible because nothing needs to change about your life for You to be brilliant. You already *are* brilliantly Being Life, naturally. Yes, your Life is perfect and nothing is ultimately wrong. You've just been buying into the conditioned belief that something was. And in doing so, your mind has been helping you to find an endless supply of things to fix so that you can, eventually, at some point in the future relax, love life and be happy. Crazy isn't it! So many people spend their entire life waiting for some future moment to fulfil them when true peace, love and happiness can only be found within their own Being now. And so they end up waiting, forever, for something that only ever exists now.

Your being is closer than your next breath. It is patiently waiting to be savoured and loved.

One of the most marvellous aspects of resting in being is the discovery that you are not separate from love and that it is very natural for you to ...

CHAPTER FIVE

Live in Love
· · · ·
INNER TEACHING FOUR

Be *One* With The
Purest Power On The Planet

LOVE IS THE ESSENCE OF YOUR BEING. Believe it or not, love is *what you are*. It is not something you *get* depending on what you *do*, but an inner presence that is experienced when you are *being you now*. The amount of love you experience has very little to do with how much affection you *get* from other people or how good your life circumstances happen to be. Quite the opposite in fact! You experience Love by resting in your Being and in the here and now, being open to *give* love fully. As a result, there is no upper limit on the amount of love that you can experience in this lifetime.

Love Is Absolutely Infinite + Ever-Present.
Unconditional love is the only love that exists. Love is an experience that exists beyond the mind because it is beyond expectations, judgments, reasons, justifications and conditions, and beyond time. Love is perfect, whole and complete and is always present.

> *Love is like air. It is present throughout your day, even if at times you aren't aware of it existing. And like air, love supports life, without needing anything in return.*

The level of love you enjoy depends upon how much love you give. Relationships tend to break down when one or both people involved withdraw from giving love. The main thing that limits the love you give is the set of mind-based conditions you (unintentionally) place upon what is required for yourself, other people and life to be deemed loveable. These conditions act as "hoops" that people and life circumstances have to jump through in order to warrant your love.

> *To love unconditionally is to fully embrace the moment you're in.*

"I'll love myself when I get accepted onto my college course" or "I'll love myself when I graduate." "I'll be loveable when I meet someone who loves me." "I'll love myself when this, when that …" Notice the reasons that you may have unintentionally invented for not loving yourself as you are now. "I'll love other people when I've known them long enough, when they've proven themselves to me, when they're more fun, better looking, more popular …" Notice the reasons you may give yourself for not loving other people as they are now. "I'll love my life when I've improved my bank balance, left my job, grown my business …" again, notice the conditions that your mind has created, which can all be limiting the love you get to enjoy.

Learning to Love without Limits
Now it doesn't take a genius to appreciate that the more of these conditions you have, the less love you will ultimately enjoy, and the fewer conditions, the more love you naturally experience. The even better news is that these conditions all exist in your mind and the mind can be both changed and transcended.

Learn how to love things perfectly instead of trying to find perfect things to love.

In his book *Awareness*, Anthony De Mello writes, *"We are not here to change the world, we are here to love it."* The power of this statement is profound. In only a few words he takes the focus away from us trying to change the external world and places the power and responsibility instead in our own hands; specifically, in our willingness to learn how to love fully. Incidentally, I would also suggest that you are not here to change yourself, but instead, to learn how to love yourself fully, exactly as you are.

Do you love yourself unconditionally? Use the "Love Levels" Tool on page 146 to explore this question.

What would happen if you simply let go of all conditions and allowed yourself to love yourself completely, for all that you are, now?

Loving yourself is a choice you can only make now. Not when you achieve this, that or the next thing, but now! Let yourself be enough as you are. Loving the people in your life is also a choice you make now. Not when they've done this, that or the next thing, but now! Let others be enough as they are. And again, loving your life circumstances is a decision you can only ever make now. Not when things are different, better or perfect, only ever now!

Genuine unconditional love has no rules, no claiming, no ownership, no judgements, no expectations and no conditions. You simply love yourself, others and life circumstances, without needing specific reasons. You love all things now. The moment reasons come into play, you attach conditions to love. In order for you to love unconditionally, let go of having to have any logical reasons to love and let life be enough, exactly as it is.

> *Stop loving people, places, events or things "because"*
> *and let them be. Stop waiting to love things when they*
> *are different. Everything just is and unconditional love*
> *embraces all.*

Trust that your life exists to teach you how to love. Everything in your life right now, and by that I mean your current career, relationships, finances and so on, are all set up perfectly to help you learn how to love fully, and in doing so, to embrace the magnificent moment you're in.

> *If you want to love your time on Earth, which if you're*
> *reading this book I can only assume you do, then let go of*
> *conditions.*

Play with exploring what it is like to be completely fresh and innocent with the people in your life. See them with fresh eyes. Let go of any preconceived ideas you may have about your partner, parent(s), family members, friends and colleagues. Just be with them fully, giving them 100% of your attention. As if it is the first and last time you will get to be in their company. Don't try to manipulate any specific outcome from the interactions. Be open to whatever naturally wants to occur.

Pretend there is no past. You have no history with anyone. Pretend that the people in your life are perfect exactly as they are; that they just want to be happy, experience peace and know they are loved. Your "soul task" is to interact with people with fewer judgments or expectations. Don't wait for someone else to love you before you love them. You might be the very person in *their* life to show them how to love more unconditionally. Be the light that guides others home to the heart.

Let Go of Resisting Love

You may feel resistance to loving yourself. If you do, then notice and accept the resistance and let it go by remembering you are a human being, not a human doing. Therefore, you don't have to *do* anything to love yourself or to be loved, except be you now. You are amazing exactly as you are, without changing a thing. You are a miracle.

Unconditional love lets you be free to enjoy your gift of life without defining or labelling (and subsequently restricting) what may come of it. It opens you up to experiencing abundant levels of love because, as I mentioned earlier, you enjoy more love when you *give* more love away.

Embracing the new is not about being, doing or having more things, but is instead about developing a capacity to love all things now.

What is it going to take for you to choose to let your life be good enough as it is now, and feel the joy that comes from making such a life-changing decision? Are you waiting until you have more money, until more people love you, or until you get a different job title on your business card? Are you waiting until you've finished reading this book? What are you waiting for? What conditions have you attached to when you can be content with yourself, other people and your life circumstances? What if you stopped waiting and chose to notice, appreciate and enjoy all the beauty that is around you right now? What if you stopped thinking about other times and instead allowed yourself to melt into this magnificent moment? What happens when you let things be?

To truly embrace the new, you need to get out of your head and get into the moment. Reread that sentence because it is perhaps the most important one you've read so far. Get out of your head and get into the moment. How? Stop listening to your judgemental thoughts. Stop labelling your life as either good or bad, better or worse. Simply tune in to your senses. Observe everything you can see, hear, feel, smell and taste in this precious moment. Whatever is happening, simply notice it, appreciate it, enjoy it and move on to the next new moment with the intention to notice, appreciate and enjoy.

As you embrace the new, you become more at peace, able to listen to your inner wisdom and act upon it. You don't react to events based upon past conditioning or future fears. Instead, you live authentically, choosing how you want to be now.

The Solution to Problems Exists Within

Moving on from finding more love in your life is to discover the love that exists within your own heart. It is so important to explore the Inner Source of Love because I've observed that "living out of love" (i.e. unaware of the source of love within you), is one of the main causes of many physical conditions, emotional issues and life difficulties.

Based upon hundreds of Mind Detox consultations that I've conducted at my clinics and retreats, I've observed one core belief that sits at the heart of most people's problems. Namely: the belief that they are separate from the source of love and therefore have to *do* something to *be* loveable or "get" love. This belief, which is usually formed early on in life, makes people look for love on the outside. They believe they have to prove their loveability by looking and acting a certain way. And even if they do get love from external sources, they often end up being disappointed. Not because they aren't loved, but because the "outside love" is never as intimate or as fulfilling as the love found within their own hearts.

> *"Loneliness is not cured by human company. Loneliness is cured by contact with reality."*
>
> — *ANTHONY DE MELLO*

Journey Inward to Love

Everything changes when you know You are Love.

By journeying inward to find the source of love, fear falls away, along with lack, limitation or loneliness. You don't need other people to love you. You worry less about what people think of you. You know love cannot be taken away. Therefore you love with an open palm, without grasping or attachment. Relationships are given the space they need to evolve and be cherished.

> *You spend your days Being in Love with every person you meet because you've thrown away the rulebook of requirements for what has to happen for you to experience love now.*

When I say, "Being in Love," I don't mean romantic love. Through being inwardly aware you learn how to rest in your Being, which *is* love. In doing so, you live aware of the beautiful still silent presence of the divine that has never left you. It becomes clear that the presence that you are experiencing is love: unbounded, undiluted, unconditional love. Even more miraculously, when you rest fully aware of the presence of still silent love, you live free.

A Marvellous Way to Live

Beyond the conditioned mind, you are beyond beliefs, beyond limitations, beyond judgments, beyond separation, beyond problems and beyond the past or future. You are present, peaceful and experience an inner perfection right now.

Seeing the world with awe-filled eyes, you welcome life, however it may look. You no longer resist life if it doesn't turn out exactly how you think it should. Happiness naturally flows and you feel fulfilled in the knowledge that this moment lacks nothing. So let's never get distracted from our main purpose for being on this planet – to learn how to love fully.

To live in love is to directly experience the source of love within you. It is the master key that opens the door of abundance, of joy and of peace in your life and in the wider world. It is a marvellous way to live. You experience your Self as a love that is eternally present and absolutely infinite.

CHAPTER SIX

Resistance Is Futile

• • • •

INNER TEACHING SIX

Everything Happens To Help You

THINKING ABOUT THINGS AS PROBLEMS PREVENTS YOU FROM SEE-ING THE MIRACLES THAT ARE ALWAYS OCCURRING. Not only that, but problem-based thinking also slows your evolution, limits your joy and causes unnecessary stress and suffering.

> *Letting go of problems requires you to accept that nothing has meaning except for the meaning you give it. That life is what you think it is.*

When you stop engaging in judgemental thinking, people, places, events and things stop being problems. You stop needing to ma-nipulate the moment by forcing your will, allowing for a more lib-erated way of living to reveal itself. You discover that the more you have to manipulate life so it is how you *think* it should be, the less free you are. Conversely, the more you learn to be at peace with life exactly as it is, the more freedom you enjoy.

Is a Problem until You Think It Is

Whether something is a problem or not is merely a matter of opinion.

One person loses their job and experiences stress, fear and anxiety. Another person loses their job and is excited about the new possibilities opening up for them. What's the difference? The external life circumstance is the same. However the internal response is different. Enjoying a life free from problems comes from seeing that whether something is a problem or not depends on the inner labels you attach to external events. Or, in other words, that your relationship with life depends on the inner thoughts you are having *about* your life.

You cannot control everything that happens in life, but you can improve how you relate to what happens.

Mind Makes Meaning

One of the functions of your mind is to help you make sense of reality by attaching meaning to whatever happens each moment. Your mind is like an iceberg; only a small part of it sits above the surface of conscious awareness. The majority of it exists below the surface of awareness – within realms of the mind that you are not aware of during daily life. Your unconscious mind, the part of your mind that you're not aware of, takes the raw data about external events collected via your five senses. It then attaches meaning to the data gathered based upon your beliefs, values, thinking patterns, past experiences and other factors. Once it's done this filtering process, it then passes a vastly edited version of reality up to your conscious awareness.

All of this means that you don't experience things as they are, but instead experience an edited version of reality, based upon the way your unconscious mind filters reality.

Problems in the Mind, not in the Moment

It has been said: *"no mind = no problem"* because without your mind forming a judgmental opinion about what's happening, everything just is. It isn't good or bad, right or wrong, or better or worse. It just is! For something to become a problem you need to judge it as bad, worse or wrong. Explore how you might be putting your life in a judgemental box with "The Judgement Game" Tool on page 147.

> *The people, places, events and things that you perceive to be problems are not the actual problem. Instead, the real problem is you leaving the magnificent moment, judging what is as wrong and then resisting what isn't how you think it should be.*

Immense freedom comes from rising above the judgemental opinions of your conditioned mind. By doing so, you can discover how, in the main, the actions of other people along with the circumstances you encounter are ultimately neutral within themselves – neither good nor bad.

Instead, it is ultimately *your* mind-based interpretations of life, combined with your subsequent acceptance or resistance, that determines whether things are problems or not.

> *There is a difference between what's happening in reality and what you think is happening. What you think about life is only your opinion.*

When you really get this, you become able to choose whether you judge life negatively and in the process, experience pain. Or choose to suspend judgement and enjoy the peace that comes from engaging with life via a more enlightened perspective.

To Resist Life Is to Resist Miracles

The moment you stop resisting what is and start accepting the moment you're in, all your perceived problems instantly start helping you.

Everything that happens each day does so to help you move towards and create the life you want. Granted, this is not always obvious at first glance! But if you suspend judgement for long enough, you will see how miraculous life always is. Remain open-minded and you can discover that *every* life event is a signpost pointing you in the direction of what you need to learn to love in order to experience your heart's greatest desire.

To resist what happens is to resist the very things that you need in order to get what you want!

Stress, pain and negative emotions all come from resisting what is. When you stop resisting and start accepting, you immediately release the blockages built up due to your resistance and allow creativity and compassion to help your joyful self out to play. To start exploring more creative ways of thinking about your perceived problems please check out the "Getting Unstuck", "Situation Reframe", "Quantum Thinking" and "Letting Go" Tools on pages 148-152.

If you ever have a problem, ask yourself:
What am I judging and what am I resisting?

All problems are the direct result of you judging whether things are how you think they *should* be, or not. This is because when you judge things, you make it possible for certain things to be deemed "bad". The result of such a judgement can be to resist the things that you've judged as "bad", causing yourself stress. If you want to let go of problems, for good, then stop judging people, places, events and things as either good or bad and instead, accept everyone and everything for all that they are, now.

Judging requires you to have expectations about how you think things should be. Expectations are based upon the past or future. What if you let go of your expectations, allowed yourself to stop struggling against what's happening and embraced all now?

To judge the moment you're in as either "good" or "bad", you need to go into the past or future to find a reference point on which to base your judgement. In doing so you leave the magnificent moment and postpone your joy. Even if you judge the moment as being good, you can still postpone your joy, because your judgement is in the mind and your mind doesn't know what true joy is. Remember, joy exists outside your head, in the direct experience of the moment.

Own Your Opinions
If you do choose to judge things, then own your judgements. Avoid making sweeping statements about *how things are*, as if they are universal truths that everyone should believe. Instead, make it clear

that it is your opinion of what you personally think and feel, remaining aware that it is only *your* interpretation. For instance, the coffee shop doesn't make bad coffee, you just happen to prefer coffee made a different way! Your boss isn't bad; you would just prefer them to act differently.

By owning your judgements, you reduce your resistance to what is because you are aware that your judgements are only your opinions about things, not what everyone *should* think and agree to or how things *must* be. You also recognize that because they are *your* judgements, you are the only person that can do anything about how you feel about what's happening. That you can instantly stop all pain caused by things not being how you think they should be. Instead, you make choices and take actions in accordance with what it is you want while remaining open-minded as to whether what's happening is good or bad.

Good or Bad, Who Knows!

Once upon a time there was an old wise man who owned a lovely horse. Then one day, out of the blue, his horse broke free and ran away. A neighbour who heard what happened said: "That is terrible news that your only horse ran away." However, the wise man replied, "Good or bad, who knows!"

Miraculously a week later the man's horse returned, bringing with it ten wild stallions. Witnessing the spectacular scene, the neighbour said, "That's great news that you now have ten new stallions." To which the wise man replied, "Good or bad, who knows!"

A few days later the son of the wise man was out training one of the new stallions when he was thrown off, landed badly and broke his leg. The concerned neighbour said, "That's terrible news that your son broke his leg." The wise man responded just as he had before, saying, "Good or bad, who knows!"

Two more weeks past and then the army came to town, enrolling all the young men to go fight in the war. The son couldn't fight because of his leg. And yes, you guessed it, the wise man had the same open-minded response: "Good or bad, who knows!"

I love this parable because it so beautifully illustrates what this part of the book is all about. When things happen in life you never know for certain at the time if they are good or bad. And if you are patient, you will more often than not appreciate when looking back on events that they were the best possible things to happen. Or put a different way, miracles are always happening, even if at the time we don't always recognize them as such. To apply this to past events that you have perceived as problems, please use the "Hindsight Helps" Tool on page 153 in Appendix 1.

> *"Sometimes not getting what you think you want is a wonderful stroke of luck."*
>
> — *DALAI LAMA*

Bring It On!

One of the most powerful affirmations for living a problem-free existence is simply: *"Bring it on!"* This phrase works so effectively because it requires exactly the opposite mindset to resistance.

> *"Bring it on!" is a potent antidote to any problem.*

For instance, the negative emotion of fear is a common problem that stops people going for what they want. What's important to know about fear is that it requires resistance in order for it to be a problem. Or in other words, fear needs you to *not want to feel it* in order for it to have any power over you. By saying *"Bring it on!"* to the feeling of fear, you may find that it immediately loses its power.

Personally, I find that when I say *"Bring it on!"* to fearful feelings they immediately transform into enlivening energy; a powerful inner strength that I can use to help me be more alert and focused and perform better than I would have without the initial feelings. Fear, which used to be a big problem for me, has become a friend rather than a foe. Explore this yourself using the "Freedom from Fear"Tool on page 154.

> *You can accept things so that you are no longer resisting them and still take action to make things how you would prefer them to be.*

The difference is that when you accept things, you stop resisting them and no longer experience them as problematic. When you own your judgements and accept that all pain is caused by your resistance to what is, you will find that your joyfulness is nothing to do with your bank balance, your relationships or your job. Instead, your joyfulness is everything to do with accepting what's happening now.

Stop Benefiting from Problems

Benefiting from having problems is one of the biggest barriers to letting go of them for good. To stop making things into problems, you need to be aware of how you may have been benefiting from *not* letting go of them before now.

> *Benefit from getting bored by your problems.*

Consider this for each problem: What is it that you're doing that you enjoy doing, but won't be able to do when your problem disappears? What are you not doing and what will you *have to do* when you let go of the problem? Do the problems give you something to talk about with your friends and family? When chatting to others about the difficulties you're having, do you give each other love, support and advice?

> *Problems can provide you with purpose to your day and meaning to your life, giving you something to think about, talk about and "solve". Letting go of problems could produce a gap.*

Explore this: What would happen if all your problems ceased to exist and you had nothing to solve? What would you do with your day if everything were perfect, if *you* were perfect? What would you talk about? What would you do? Stop. Take as long as you need to answer one of the most important questions you may ever ask yourself: *What would you do if you had absolutely NO problems?* Your answer could be the difference between whether you recreate problems for the rest of your life or choose to stop living in the illusion of problems, stop creating unnecessary pain for yourself and instead, live a problem-free existence from this moment on.

> *When you embrace the new, you find there is no gap needing to be filled because the gap is now. By giving your attention to this moment you are fulfilled.*

Life is now. You create your life every moment. If you have a problem, you have created it now by thinking about it in your mind. If you still have the same problem as you did a moment ago, then you have recreated it again in this moment. And yes, you guessed it, if you still have the same problem as you had three moments ago, then you've recreated it again!

Why would you keep recreating problems? Explore this question using the "Hidden Benefits" Tool on page 156. Perhaps you haven't learnt what you need to learn in order to overcome them all? Now, you could spend years trying to figure out all the logical learning for every problem you think you've ever had, or you can choose to stop thinking about things as problems. If you do, then your life circumstances may stay the same, but they stop being a problem. Start thinking about things as problems again, start resisting again and you get problems again. It can be as simple as that.

Choose a Problem-Free Existence

You have the power to create and un-create problems in an instant. So let go of problems. Accept what is and take actions that reflect what you want.

No external person or event has the inherent power to negatively impact your inner experience of life. It is only your conditioned mind that will convince you otherwise. It is not what's happened, is happening or might happen that is causing your inner emotions, but instead, it is your internal thinking about external life. The truth is that it is possible to raise your level of consciousness to a point where you don't experience anything as a problem.

When living in a more conscious way you actively choose the meaning that you give to life events. Remember, events are events; they are not good, not bad. They are unable to emotionally impact you in a negative way – unless you *think* they are problems. Instead of unconsciously attaching meaning to events, you can consciously choose the meaning you want. The consequences of this shift are massive because they will make your life circumstances irrelevant to your life enjoyment.

You live a "joy-full" life rather than a "problem-full" life
by choosing the meaning you attach to events.

Letting go of problems is not about denying reality; it's recognizing that you create your own version of reality. If you no longer want to have problems, then choose to create a problem-free reality. Work on things as and when they require your attention. Make choices in the now in line with what you want and then move on to embrace the next new thing and then the next. To live this way is to live consciously by embracing your evolution.

Acceptance Speeds Up Your Evolution

If life must only happen how you think it should, then you limit life from being any other way. Evolution needs you to be open to *be* things you've never been, *know* things you've never known and *do* things you've never done. Resisting what's happening because it doesn't match what you think should happen holds on to the past and fears the future; the unexpected. Evolution loves the moment you're in and embraces the unexpected. Accepting life in whatever direction it flows enables you to grow, explore and deal with events as they happen, efficiently, effectively and effortlessly.

When you stop judging and resisting and start accepting, life is joyful. You have no anger because there is nothing to be angry about. You hold no grudges. You never need to forgive because there is never anything to forgive. You have no guilt because there is nothing to feel guilty about. You have no frustration. No hurt. No stress. You are thankful for what happens as it helps you to grow and become more enlightened. You stop swimming upriver. You let miracles flow.

Allow yourself to flow by celebrating your evolution.

CHAPTER SEVEN

Compromise Corrodes

. . . .

INNER TEACHING SEVEN

Be Heroic By Following Your Heart

HAVING THE COURAGE TO BE GUIDED BY YOUR HEART LEADS TO A MIRACULOUS LIFE LIBERATED FROM COMPROMISE. On the other hand, if you make choices and carry out actions out of fear or obligation, then you can find yourself becoming tired, frustrated and resentful and, as a direct consequence, prevent good things from entering your life. The trick is to know the difference between helpful and harmful compromise, then be heroic by being, doing and having what makes your heart sing.

A compromise-free life is a free life indeed.

The Compromise that Corrodes

Some compromises in life are helpful because they offer opportunities for you to surrender your ego-based desires. By this I mean that helpful compromises allow you to step beyond the confines of your mental conditioning to enjoy unexpected life experiences that are very enlivening for your soul.

However, there is also a kind of compromise that can be quite literally soul-destroying. Unhealthy compromise happens when you consistently be, do or have things that are in direct conflict with what your heart knows is best. Or in other words, harmful compromises happen when you know something is not right for you, but you continue with it anyway.

Harmful compromise creates inner conflict that corrodes your peace and suppresses your joy.

Head–Heart Conflict

Compromise makes you play small and buy into the illusion that you cannot have what you ultimately want. Problems are perceived and miracles are prevented if you consistently ignore your heart by opting to rely too heavily on your head.

Within your heart exists an inner wisdom that can guide you, if you let it.

The thing you must understand about compromise is that no end of intellectual convincing can ever prevail over the deep and immediate knowing of your heart. As a result, it doesn't matter how much intellectual convincing you attempt to engage in; if you are compromising, then your heart can never be fooled. With that in mind, I invite you to be heroic now by asking yourself this question:

Where in my life am I compromising?

This question is so incredibly powerful because it highlights any area(s) of your life where you are currently in conflict with your heart. You will find when asking this question that you know any compromises almost immediately. Talking of which, when you read the above question, did a particular relationship or life circumstance pop into your mind? If not, maybe an eating or drinking habit did? Irrespective of what came to mind, this question is not an opportunity for you to beat yourself up, but instead, a chance to lift yourself up by realigning yourself with your heart and exploring how to eradicate harmful compromise from your life.

Permission to Put Yourself First

Consider this: If you aren't healthy, how are you going to help anyone else to be healthy? If you aren't at peace, how are you going to help someone else be at peace? And if you aren't contented, how are you going to help other people be contented?

Putting yourself first is about living authentically. When you are authentic, you are in harmony with yourself and your surroundings. You don't want one thing, but out of obligation do something else. You are at peace because there is no inner conflict. With no inner conflict you open yourself up for miracles to flow through you. To meet the universe halfway you ask for and focus upon what you want, while giving other people the freedom to do the same. You make choices and take actions that are consistent with what feels right for you. Use the "Observing Obligations" Tool on page 156 in Appendix 1 to find out where in your life you are doing things because you think you should.

Putting Yourself First Is Not Selfish

"Do yourself a favour by doing someone else one" is some of the best advice ever given to me by my spiritual teacher. Since applying it with my heart, mind, body and soul I've found that service can be one of the quickest paths of evolution and eternal joy.

Helping someone without expecting anything in return reaps rapid rewards. Quite simply, it makes you feel fantastic! You get your mind out of the way and live from love. You don't do things because you feel obligated to do so; instead, you serve others because it brings you so much joy. It's about making choices and taking actions with loving intent, rather than obligation.

When you put yourself first you love yourself unconditionally. You don't seek validation by external means or try to convince other people that you're good enough to be loved. You don't seek possessions and power to justify your existence or try to impress. You don't present yourself as somebody important or show how smart you are. Instead, you are peaceful and able to listen to and follow your inner wisdom. You enjoy incredibly loving relationships because you stop selling yourself, start *being* yourself and in the process attract people into your life who love you for who you are. You don't fear what others think of you or what might happen in your life circumstances because you don't identify yourself with external life factors. Naturally, you respect yourself, respect other people and respect the world you live in.

Be and Do What *You* Love!

Curing corrosive compromise is about asking for what you want and never feeling obligated to be, do and have things that are in conflict with your heart. You put yourself first. You may need to give yourself permission to do this. If you feel any resistance to putting yourself first, notice it, accept it and be willing to let it go. Have the courage to say "no" to the things that you don't want. Do the things you enjoy so much that you lose track of time doing them. Paint. Sing. Dance. Say "yes" to being, doing and having all the things that make your heart sing.

CHAPTER EIGHT

Prioritize Praise

· · · ·

INNER TEACHING EIGHT

The Power Of Praise Prevails Over Problems

APPRECIATION IS THE KEY TO THE TREASURE CHEST OF AMAZING GIFTS THAT ARE ALREADY PRESENT IN YOUR LIFE. Your life, in whatever shape or form it's taking at this moment, *is your life*. Without it, you'd be dead. So embrace it! You are alive. Accept your gift of life with open arms and be grateful for it every moment. Without acceptance you close your mind off to all the miracles this universe is endlessly giving you.

> *Notice, appreciate and enjoy what you already have to embrace your true wealth.*

Focusing on what you're not, can't do and don't have will lead to an unenlightened life consisting of suffering and scarcity, where you spend your days trying to be different, wishing you had more. Instead, make the decision to be appreciative.

Praise Prevails over Problems

Being praiseful is the ultimate antidote to problems. By praise, I don't mean anything religious. Rather, I'm referring to a very natural way of being whereby you are genuinely grateful about being alive. Praise, which is the doorway to appreciation, is a choice you can make at any moment. Irrespective of what's happening, it is always possible to make it a priority to be in a state of praise instead of criticism.

Let me prove it to you now. Wherever you happen to be as you read these words, I want you to stop and have a look around. While you do, I want you to find something that you do NOT like. *(I know it's not a very positive thing for me to ask you to do, but bear with me, we are going somewhere!).* Do your best to find something within your current setting to criticize. Then, once you've found it, take a few moments to actively think critical comments about it in your mind. You might notice a stain on the carpet, a pile of dirty clothes that need to be washed, or hear the music that you don't like coming from your neighbour's place. Find something now and think critical thoughts about it for a few moments. As you do, notice what happens within your body.

Anyone I've ever done this exercise with has commented that they have felt a heaviness or constriction in their body and described a range of other downward-spiralling emotional experiences.

Now, with the *exact same thing* you were just being negative about, I want you to find something to praise about it. I appreciate that you may have to scrape the bottom of the barrel and be creative, but nevertheless, for a few moments I want you to actively think positive and praiseful comments about it in your mind.

So you could now choose to be appreciative of having a carpet that keeps your house warm, clothes to wear and fully functioning ears that are able to hear sounds.

Again, as you do, notice what happens within your body. If you genuinely do rise above the previous negative comments by focusing on what you can praise, you will find that a change occurs within your psyche. The feedback I consistently receive when asking people to do this includes that they feel lighter, more open and expansive.

Overall, the comments I get are that praising is an upward-spiralling emotional experience, in contrast to criticizing. Now here's the point. Miraculously, the thing you were originally criticizing did NOT have to change for your inner experience of it to improve – your experience changed and improved simply through the power of praise. Apply this to your own life now, using the "Choosing Praise"Tool on page 157 in Appendix 1.

Freedom from Problems Is a Choice

This simple praise game perfectly illustrates a liberating possibility when it comes to enjoying freedom from problems for good. It proves that your emotional experience of life is ultimately your choosing. By "experience of life", I don't mean the external events occurring because they can often be outside your direct control. However, your inner experience of life can always be a positive one if you choose to make it a priority to praise. Take a moment to consider the implications of this. Your external life circumstances, whether on the surface they appear to be good or bad, no longer need to have any power over how good you feel inside.

Freedom in life comes from you being OK irrespective of what's happening. If you have to manage and control your life so that it looks exactly how you think it should, then you aren't free. Quite the opposite! Your emotional experience of life will continue to be governed by external forces because your mood will go up and down depending on inner thinking about the weather of your life circumstances. In fact, the truth is that you can only be free by learning to let life be. You don't have to wait for your life circumstances to improve before you can experience your heart's greatest desire. You can be happy now!

With the power of praise you enter into a state of joyful existence, flowing from one moment to the next, effortlessly enjoying the journey.

CHAPTER NINE

Positive Focus
Has Power

· · · ·

INNER TEACHING NINE

You Are A Natural-Born Miraclemaker

YOU ARE ALREADY A NATURAL-BORN MIRACLEMAKER. There isn't a moment that goes by when you are not already, like magic, attracting what you focus on into your life. You do it naturally, often without realizing, all of the time. Stop to reflect upon your current life situation, and you will notice that your life is the physical manifestation of what you've been thinking about most over the past few days, weeks, months or years. Your relationships, career, finances, health and happiness will all be a reflection of your focus.

Out of habit, people often focus their attention on the things that they don't have or don't want, rather than what they already have and what they want. However, you move towards and become what you focus on the most. If you focus on the things you don't want, sooner or later you'll end up creating what you don't want! You may be worried about money or feel alone or trapped by responsibilities. You may think you have complicated family relations, or be of the opinion that you're in the wrong job. However, if you focus on the things you don't want, you will continue to get the things you don't want.

If you aren't enjoying how magnificent you and other people are and the world is, then change your focus.

THINGS YOU DON'T WANT	THINGS YOU DO WANT
Conflict	Peace
Scarcity	Abundance
Imperfection	Perfection
Anxiety	Ease
Unloved	Love
Fear	Courage
Uncertainty	Certainty
Guilt	Self-Acceptance
Sadness	Joy
Trapped	Freedom
Loneliness	Connection
Unconfident	Confidence
Worry	Faith

Become aware of what you're focusing on, and ask:
What do I want?

Are you focusing on conflict, when you want peace? Are you focusing on scarcity, when you want abundance? Are you focusing on fear, when you want courage? Make it your daily practice to be aware of what you are focusing on. If you ever notice yourself thinking about things you don't want, then gently change your focus. Doing so will not only help to bring what you want into your life, but will also make you feel more positive because you feel what you focus on.

> *Remember, you move towards and become what you focus on the most. Focus on abundance. Focus on love. Focus on peace. Focus on joy. Focus on freedom. Focus on what you want.*

A More Effective Way to Use Your Mind

Positive focus also allows your unconscious mind to help you to become aware of all the things you need in order to get what you want. This is because there are aspects of your mind that operate above the surface of consciousness (thoughts you are aware of) and a part of your mind that operates below the surface of consciousness that you are not aware of.

> *Your conscious mind is the goal-setter whereas your unconscious mind is the goal-getter.*

Although you may consciously consider what it is you want, it is actually your unconscious mind that is going to help you to get it. Here's how it works: Your unconscious mind gathers a huge amount of information about your external environment, but only passes a small percentage of the gathered data up to your conscious awareness, making your conscious experience of life a vastly edited version.

To help you understand the implications of this internal filtering process I invite you to imagine that you are outside and it's raining heavily. Every second about 400 billion droplets of rain fall from the sky and every second you reach out and catch just a handful of the raindrops, approximately 2000 droplets. In this analogy, you are only consciously aware of the raindrops that land on your hand and not of the billions of raindrops that are falling all around. The same is true for your version of reality.

To help you avoid being overwhelmed, your unconscious mind only lets you become aware of what it believes is important and relevant to you. Your focus is a key determinant of what things "land on your hand" i.e. those that you are aware of, and what things "fall to the ground" without you being consciously aware of them ever existing.

Positive focus allows your mind to help you to become consciously aware of all of the people, places, events and things that will help you get what you want.

Living with Loving Intent
Leading on from focus is your intent. Your intention is the sum of all the more subtle reasons behind why you want what you think you want. Your intent influences the choices you make and how you feel and behave in each moment. Your intent also influences what you get because even though your focus might be positive, if your intentions are negative you can end up attracting the emotionally charged negative intention rather than the positive desire.

For two years I had the desire to meet a life partner. I was focusing on the kind of person I'd like to be in a relationship with, but was confused as to why I hadn't met anyone yet. After a conversation with my coach I discovered that, although I wanted to meet someone, my intent for doing so was so that I wasn't lonely any more. Further more, I had much more emotion attached to *not* being lonely than to the idea of being in a relationship. As a consequence, I was consistently and unconsciously attracting loneliness into my life, despite focusing on meeting someone.

Miraculously, after getting the negative intentions out into the open and making sure that my intent was positive, I left the coaching session and that same afternoon met a wonderful woman with whom I ended up enjoying a wonderful relationship for the next few years. True story!

Now, could *your* intentions be stopping you from attracting miracles? Use the "Loving Intent" Tool on page 158 to find out how pure your intentions are.

Ask yourself, what do I want? Then ask yourself, why do I want it? Doing so can help you to determine whether your intent is fear or love-based.

CONSIDER THIS: Why do you want to meet a life partner? Do you want to enjoy a deep connection with another human being or are you trying to avoid being lonely? Why do you want more money? Is it so you don't end up being stuck in a job you hate? Notice your intentions. As you will get your emotionally charged intentions, you will get loneliness if your intent is to avoid it. You will get no money if you try to avoid having no money. Your goals can be anything; just make sure your intent is loving and focus on what you want.

When you embrace the new, let go of problems and focus on what you want, your intent naturally changes. You are joyful, have nothing to prove and appreciate that life is a gift to be celebrated. As a result, your intent is different to if you pursued things with fear-based intentions, such as to avoid loneliness or be valued by others. Your goals may stay the same, but your intent is different. You are no longer trying to avoid pain and feel better. Instead, your intent for being, doing and having things comes from a place of love. Remember, you move towards and become what you focus on the most. You will attract your intentions.

*Make choices and take actions with loving intent towards
yourself, other people and the world.*

Your Mind Moves towards Happiness

Linking negative emotions with what you want can stop you from
getting them. I appreciate it may seem odd for me to suggest that
you would ever intentionally feel bad about creating positive outcomes, but you would be amazed by how often it actually happens.

When people think about what they want, they can end up
feeling bad because they don't have it yet. This can block what you
want because it is the natural tendency of your mind to move you
towards greater happiness. By linking negative emotions with your
goals, your mind can end up moving you away from getting them
in an innocent attempt to help you avoid unhappiness. To become
a magnet for miracles it is thus vitally important that you link positive emotions with your goals. Or, in other words, that you enjoy
your future now.

Mind the Gap

*Setting goals creates a gap between where you are now
and where you anticipate being in the future.*

When you decide that you want something different to what you
currently have, you immediately create a gap between where you
are now and where you want to be. This gap can cause you to put
more of your attention on doing, rather than resting in being. It
can also cause you to resist *what is* and create discontent by focusing on how things are not how you want them to be. These
negative feelings often become associated with your future goals,

making your mind work to avoid them as opposed to obtain them. Furthermore, to feel better you can end up struggling to change your circumstances and become so focused on the future that you end up missing the magnificent moment you're in.

When attracting miracles, be aware of and accept the gap, appreciate the moment you're in and choose actions consistent with the reality you want.

Emotions: The Link between Two Worlds

The universe is made up of energy. Look around and you will see energy in many different forms. Everything is made up of it. Including the things you want. Your emotions are energy in **motion**. They are one of the first ways your thoughts become manifested into physical reality.

Emotions are the link between non-manifested thoughts and manifested physical reality. They are therefore a very powerful tool in your miracle-manifesting toolkit.

Out of all of the emotions, praise, gratitude and love are the most powerful. The more you live in accordance with these upward-spiralling emotional experiences, the more your path naturally turns to gold. Ever since I've made it a priority to live in love, be praiseful as much as possible and cultivate an attitude of gratitude, my ability to attract positive outcomes has skyrocketed. It is as though nowadays the red carpet of life rolls towards me, instead of me struggling so hard to knit my own carpet! Emotions are part of the energy that makes up the universe. To harness the power of the universe is to channel your emotions effectively.

Enjoying Your Future Now

Breathe life into what you want by appreciating it now. Tune in to your senses using your imagination. Bring to mind what you will see, hear, feel, smell and taste when you have attracted what you want. Be still and appreciate your future now, as if it has already been manifested. How would you feel? What would you be saying to yourself? How amazing will it be to bring about this positive change to your life? Appreciate it now.

> *When you appreciate what you want now, you naturally enjoy your journey towards your goals.*

Falling into the trap of attempting to feel certain ways by achieving certain things is common. However, this puts your feelings on hold and places your life enjoyment at the mercy of whether you achieve your goals or not.

Enjoying the journey is about no longer trying to feel certain ways by doing or having certain things. It is about appreciating that every feeling you could ever experience comes from within, is within you now, waiting to be given permission to flow around your body. Remember, due to the miraculous mind–body connection you feel what you focus on. Nothing can make you feel any way except what you put your focus on. Any time you experience a feeling, whether it is sadness or joy, you are the one who has created it. You have the power to create any feelings you want. For more guidance see the "Creating States" Tool on pages 159 and 160. Create the feelings you want by focusing on what you want and letting your body–mind take care of the rest.

Be appreciative of your gift of life, irrespective of life circumstances. Having an attitude of gratitude not only makes you feel great, but also enables you to manifest your goals in the most effective, effortless and enjoyable way. See page 161 for a "Gratitude Attitude" Tool to help you do this. Remember, embracing the new takes all pain out of achievement because you are flexible, accepting and joyful along the way. Letting go of thinking about things as problems enables you to take steps towards your goals without life being good or bad, better or worse or right or wrong. Instead, you live with the open-minded assumption that everything happens to help you. Life becomes a joyful adventure.

By feeling how you want to feel now, you become less attached to the things you want and, as a consequence, increase the flow of good into your life.

CHAPTER TEN

Let Go to Let Grow

• • • •

INNER TEACHING TEN

Discover The Difference Between Desire And Desperation

HARNESSING THE POWER OF THE UNIVERSE REQUIRES YOU TO COME FROM THE MOST SURRENDERED PLACE POSSIBLE. There is a direct relationship between surrendering control and manifesting miracles because of the difference between desire and desperation. Desire pulls things towards you, while desperation pushes them away. If you chase after things you *think you need* out of desperation, they will tend to run away from you. Pursuing goals with fear-based intentions, such as to avoid sadness, be valued by others or gain respect can cause you to become attached to your goals – to the point that you may think you need them. However, need implies desperation.

Know what you want, then let go of needing it.

Learning to Let Go

Attachment creeps into goal achievement if you mistakenly believe that your happiness, peace or love is dependent on external factors. If you believe that you can't be happy until you get the promotion, then you are attached. Or if you believe that you need to meet someone in order to experience love, then you are attached. Even if you get someone to love you, it will be a relationship based upon fear, not love, as you immediately become scared of losing the person you think is your source of love. Use the "Acknowledging Attachments" Tool on page 162 to ascertain if you are attached to your desires.

Attachment makes you slave to life's golden carrots.

Irrespective of what the external outcome is, if you *need it* then you are giving away your power. In the process, because you need it to make you feel happy, peaceful or loved, you can become highly controlling and manipulative in an attempt to get your own way. Attachment is exhausting! It is made worse by the fact that attachment feeds the illusionary unenlightened human experience that you are separate from peace, love and joy. You are not. All these wonderful experiences are built into the fabric of your Being (see Chapter 4).

Attachment Pushes Away Miracles
You always get what you focus on. If you become very attached to achieving goals, to the point of needing them, you can start focusing on trying to avoid *not* achieving them. Your focus on trying to avoid failing to achieve them can actually obstruct your goals from flowing into your life; you will actually be focusing on *not* achieving them. And again, this kind of focus can also shift your intent from love and abundance to fear and scarcity.

Embracing the new makes it possible to desire things without becoming attached to whether you achieve them. You can be detached and still be very determined. When detached, you take action in the moment, notice how things change and then choose new actions in the next moment. You are willing to welcome new, unexpected events and things into your life. You are embracing the new, melting into the magnificent moment and trusting that you will get what you want in the perfect way at the perfect time. To approach manifestation in this way is to have faith in the abundant nature of the universe.

When attracting what you want, never demand when you should receive as this can postpone it!

Trust that the Universe Is Never Late!

Some formulas for goal achievement tell you to be clear on when it should happen by. Although I agree it can be useful to have an idea of when – so that you stay motivated and have boundaries to work within – I strongly urge you to let go of being attached to any fixed calendar date.

Living a miraculous life is about letting go of having to get what you want within specific time frames. Instead, trust that you will get your goals at the perfect time. Quite often it is far sooner than you expect, but sometimes not. It won't matter if you are filling yourself up with the abundance of this magnificent moment. Enlightened living causes you to enjoy your journey so much that you won't have time to care if you are getting your goals or not!

By now, if you've applied what I've shared so far, you will be much more content, appreciative and fulfilled with how your life is, right now. Anything you might want in the future will have become a bonus, but not something you need to be happy, peaceful or experience love as you know these are all experiences that come from being, not doing. From this liberated problem-free perspective, you are ready to harness the power of the universe for the benefit of yourself and all of humanity.

Want It, Give It

The more you give, the more you receive.

When you throw a pebble into a pond, the ripples go out for a while until they reach the shore ... at which point they come back, multiplied in both size and quantity. The same is true for when you give in life. The more you give, the more you receive. It may seem an odd concept – to give away what you want – but you get more of what you want by giving more of what you have away.

People can live their lives by "what comes around goes around" – by not giving until they receive.

For instance, they postpone doing their best at their job until they get paid more. Or they don't show love towards other people until other people show love towards them. However, this is an ineffective strategy. By holding on to what you've got, you have no room for more to flow into your life. You end up holding back the natural flow of the universe. But if you live with a more *"what goes around comes around"* attitude, by giving what you want, then you will end up enjoying a far more abundant and fulfilling life.

Decide what you want and find ways to give it away!

Feeling unsatisfied with parts of your life usually means you aren't giving away what you want in these areas of your life. If you want affection, give your affection. If you want encouragement, give encouragement. If you want money, then share some of yours. It's as simple as that. What you give will tend to come back. It is all about the flow of giving and receiving. And remember, giving in order to receive is not giving. It's about giving without concern for getting, in the knowledge that you can afford to give it away because the universe is infinite and the universe exists within you.

"There are two ways to live your life.

One is as though nothing is a miracle.

The other is as though everything is."

ALBERT EINSTEIN

PART TWO

Manifesting Miracles

· · · ·

BY HARNESSING THE POWER
OF THE UNIVERSE

CHAPTER ELEVEN

Harness The Power of The Universe

. . . .

MANIFESTING MIRACLES

Align Your Attention With Creation

BORN WITHIN EVERY PERSON ON THE PLANET IS THE LATENT POWER TO INTENTIONALLY DIRECT CONSCIOUSNESS, transforming it from pure potentiality into physical existence. The ancient Indian texts the *Upanishads* say *"In the beginning there was the word and the word was Om."* There was a time when nothing existed, only still silent space. Then out of the nothing came something. The first movement from the un-manifest to the manifest is the vibration of Om.

Om is the vibration of creation. Om is the very first movement from stillness. It is the first sound that comes from silence. And it is the first something that comes from the nothing. Om can therefore be said to the manifest is the Om vibration.

> *Because time is not linear, in the beginning is eternally now.*

Existing beyond the physical realm is your mind. Thoughts are in essence unmanifested potentiality. They are the seeds of creation.

As a result, your thoughts are one of the most powerful tools you have to direct consciousness – taking it from still silent space into physical existence. (Wow, what a marvellous gift you have residing within you now!)

Everything you see around you that is man-made was once a thought in a person's mind. So if you want to create something new in your life, then you can do so by harnessing the power of your thoughts and of Om.

Harnessing the Power of Om

To align your attention with Om is to align your attention with the infinite power of creation. It can be incredibly powerful. Whatever thoughts you marry Om up with in your mind can help to bring them into creation.

To harness the power of Om you can create what I call an "Om Thought". If you want more love then "Om Love" would be a very powerful Om Thought to use. If you want to make more money then "Om Abundance" would be a valuable addition to your mind. Remember, you are going to marry up "Om" with a positive intention so keep your desire positive and general i.e. not Om Ferrari! If you want a new car then it would be best to use "Om Abundance". Make sure you use a purely positive concept that best summarizes in one or two words what it is you ultimately want. (Hint: Consider using your Heart's Highest Hope as your positive intention.)

For the best results, think your Om Thought with your eyes open throughout your day. Once you have thought it, simply move on with your day until the next time you want to repeat it, which might be minutes or hours later. You are not trying to force a feeling; it works even if you think or feel that it isn't working. Every time you think it you are watering the seeds of your intentions by aligning your attention with the power of the universe.

REMEMBER: The universe does not like to be manipulated. This is a very powerful technique so it must be used with loving intent.

How to Meditate Using Your Om Thought

I recommend that you do this meditation two to three times every day for about ten minutes (or more if you want). Good times of the day are before breakfast, before dinner and before bed. For closed-eye sitting meditation, use the following instructions:

STEP NO.1 **Preparation**

Sit comfortably on a seat, sofa or even on your bed. Wear comfortable clothes, support yourself with cushions and wrap yourself in a blanket if there's a chance you could get chilly. Then decide what you want to create in your life: love, peace, happiness, health, abundance, adventure or whatever.

STEP NO.2 **Gently Be Aware of Now**

Gently close your eyes while remaining alert. From the here and now, let your attention rest wide as you watch whatever is happening within your mind, right now. This takes no effort, no straining or trying. Continue by very easily, comfortably and gently observing your thoughts as they flow through your mind – as if they were passing clouds in the vast sky.

STEP NO.3 **Think Your Om Thought**

Gently think your Om Thought – "Om Love" or "Om Peace" or whatever you have chosen. After you think your Om Thought, let it go. Do not try to hold it in your mind. Just stay alert and watch whatever is happening within your awareness.

After a while you will notice that your mind has become active and that you have started thinking. This is natural and a habit, so go easy on yourself. Whenever you notice that you've been thinking, gently rethink your Om Thought. For the rest of your time meditating, go slowly between being aware, thinking your Om Thought, being aware as you wait until you start thinking, then rethinking your Om Thought, being aware … and so on. Go back and forth, in a very easy and comfortable way. There is a reminder of this process in the "Om Thought Meditation Instructions" Tool on page 163 along with another powerful "Process for Attracting Goals" Tool on page 164 that you can use to send the universe a consistent message about what you want.

It is recommended that you do the "Process for Attracting Goals" exercise at the end of your "Om Thought" meditation sitting. Doing so will give you a very powerful daily routine that can bring about miraculous changes in your life.

Transforming Your Life from the Inside Out

With regular practice you may start to notice more of what you want in your life. You may also become aware of a quietness or stillness or peace. This is your conscious awareness. It is good when meditating to let your attention move to the stillest quietest part of your inward experience so that you can cultivate a more intimate relationship with the beauty and brilliance of your unbounded conscious awareness (also known as your 'being', which was discussed early in this book). By discovering the peace, love and abundance that exists within, you naturally experience more of what you want in your external world too.

CHAPTER TWELVE

Meet The Universe Halfway

. . . .

MANIFESTING MIRACLES

Action + Patience = Success

NOW TAKE THE INNER TEACHINGS OUT INTO THE WORLD. It is not wise to sit meditating in your house all day expecting everything you want to come knocking on your door! The Ten Inner Teachings share ancient wisdom and practical exercises for creating the most positive and powerful inner platform, upon which you can take purposeful actions to build your ideal body, life and world. Applying the Ten Inner Teachings makes it an exciting adventure of creation full of love, joy and productive peace.

Now is the point when it serves to move the Ten Inner Teachings out into physical reality, or in other words, to meet the universe halfway.

Persist until You Succeed

Commitment sits at the heart of meeting the universe halfway. There will be times when things will feel as if they are flowing nicely and it's easy to enjoy the journey. However, what goes up can sometimes come down, so there may also be times when getting what you want feels more difficult. At these more challenging times it might be tempting to quit.

*Commitment turns the possibility of realizing your
dreams into an inevitability.*

Commitment requires you to do the things you said you would,
long after the positive emotions you had when you said you would
do them have left you. Commitment makes you a person of your
word. It also makes the realization of your dreams inevitable
because instead of focusing on "if" you will do it, you focus your
attention on why you want it and what you can actively do to
get it.

*The achievement of your dreams depends upon your I.Q.
level – your "I QUIT" level. What is it going to take for
you to give up on your dreams?*

Persistence is a key trait to any budding miraclemaker. If you make
the commitment that you will never quit, then success will become
inevitable for you. A genuine commitment allows for no get-out
clause, or any ifs, buts or maybes – just the total acceptance that
you will take persistent action until you succeed.

Action without Evidence
Whenever you change your body, life or world there can be a time
lag between taking action and seeing any results. Knowing this
upfront can provide you with the right mentality for staying the
distance.

Action Steps + Patience = Success

Meeting the universe halfway involves taking consistent action and
having patience. For example, if you want to grow some vegetables,

you need to get seeds, plant them in soil, water them and wait a while until they grow into the end product. The same is also the case when changing your external circumstances. For a while there may be no evidence whatsoever that anything is happening. Despite this, you need to be willing to take consistent action anyway. To gain momentum, use the "Daily Review" Tool on page 165.

Be willing to invest energy in what it is you want, even if at first you don't see obvious returns.

Energy in Action

Energy, liveliness, get-up-and-go, oomph, or whatever you like to call it, is required for making positive changes to your body, life and world.

In the same way that "like attracts like" in relationships, from the universe's perspective "life attracts life".

Energy attracts energy and what you want is made up of energy. For you to create new and wonderful things it is vital that you raise your energy to a level that matches the energy of the body, life and world that you ultimately want.

Do things that bring you energy and stop doing things that take your energy away ... is the simple, yet profound philosophy of the ancient Hawaiian Kahunas. These powerful miraclemakers and healers knew very clearly that "mana" (their word for life force or energy) is one of the most precious resources a human being has at their disposal to impact reality. Without energy you have no life and with low energy you will find it very hard to heal your body or world. In order to meet the universe halfway it is vital that you do everything within your power to keep your energy up. Explore your "Energy Sources" with the Tool on page 166 in Appendix 1 and use the following top tips to aid your energy enhancement:

TOP TIP NO. 1 Breathe for Life

Life can be sustained for weeks without food, days without water but only minutes without air. This simple fact goes to illustrate the key role that breathing plays in enhancing your energy. Unfortunately, most people don't breathe properly, which prevents the natural release of tension and places the body under unnecessary stress as it tries to operate with less oxygen than it would like.

Try this quick test: Place the palm of your hand on your stomach now and breathe in deeply, noticing what happens to your belly when you breathe in. Does it go in when you breathe in or does it expand outwards when you breathe in? For most people the stomach goes in when they breathe in, when in fact, breathing properly requires the exact opposite! For your lungs to expand fully, the diaphragm needs to drop causing the stomach to expand outwards. Practise breathing now as you read this, making sure your stomach moves outwards when you breathe in and then inwards when you exhale. Use the "Balanced Breathing" Tool on page 167 to breathe your way to higher energy levels.

TOP TIP NO. 2 Drink for Life

Drinking plenty of good-quality water aids brain function, reduces fatigue, increases the metabolism, helps your body to release toxic waste and has even been linked with lowering the risk of some cancers.

Aim to drink at least two litres of fresh spring water each day. A wise investment for your home is the installation of a water-purification system. Or if this is not possible, then at the very least buy a jug filter. If you need to buy bottled water then go for brands that use glass bottles; plastic packaging is more likely to release chemicals into the liquid. Carbonated drinks, including water, contain carbon dioxide, which tends to leach calcium from the reserves in your body so should be avoided.

Drinking enough water is a habit. Starting your day with a cup of hot water and lemon is very cleansing and following it with a freshly made juice is a great routine to adopt for setting your day up for success.

TOP TIP NO.3   Eat for Life

In his bestselling book *In Defence of Food*, Michael Pollan suggests an ancient answer to modern-day problems relating to health, fatigue and weight gain:

> *"Eat real food. Not too much. Mostly plants."*

I love this simple strategy for enhancing energy through the food you eat. By getting back to basics by making sure your meals consist mainly of energy-rich plants, you can very easily use food as the life-giving fuel that it is meant to be.

Avoid processed, chemical-loaded "dead" foods that make your body acidic and require vast amounts of energy to digest. And while you are at it, help your body even further by not giving it too much food at any one time. Doing so will leave energy in your reserves on top of that and give you a clear mind and a cleansed body that you can use to take action. For more information about diet and nutrition along with mind and body detox, please see my books *Life Detox*, *Life-Changing Weight Loss* and *Heal the Hidden Cause*.

TOP TIP NO. 4 Move for Life

Exercise is an essential element for cultivating the right mental and emotional foundation for meeting the universe halfway. When you move your body you cause the release of endorphins into your system, which makes you feel happier. Exercise is also a great way to lose weight and look great, which in many societies can put you at a definite advantage when going for your goals. Moving your body can also help you live longer as it helps to prevent chronic health conditions including heart disease and cancers.

Human bodies are designed to move. So take the stairs, walk to the shops, buy yourself a bike – anything, but get your body moving. As you build lean muscle mass your resting metabolic rate (which determines how slowly or quickly your body burns calories) can also increase, meaning that your body may start to burn more calories even when you are resting!

TOP TIP NO. 5 Rest for Life

Insomnia is a very common problem in today's world. Busy schedules, constant stimulation and increasingly stressful demands on our time are all leading to increasingly busy minds that find it hard to switch off at the end of the day. So you are not alone if you find it hard to get to sleep at night.

Night-time is one of the main times that your body uses to heal. When you are sleeping, your body is resting. When your body rests it takes the opportunity to heal and release the stored stress accumulated during your day. This is one of the reasons why you dream when you sleep; the healing activity in your body is reflected in your mind in the form of visual images.

For relief from insomnia people commonly revert to reading books, listening to the radio or watching the television to help them get to sleep. These devices are often used to help distract from the thinking mind. Unfortunately, these forms of entertainment can actually be counterproductive to getting a good night's sleep as they can cause your mind to become even more active; and even if you do get to sleep using books, radio or television, you can end up having a less restful sleep experience – for example if the content of the entertainment included material of a stressful nature.

Using meditation to help you sleep allows you to enter sleep at a deeper level, making for a deeper, more restful sleep experience.

When meditating yourself to sleep, simply lie down in your bed and use the three steps outlined in the "Om Thought Meditation Instructions" on page 163.

Instead of thinking yourself to sleep, you can use the time to be here now, rest in being, let go of the thinking mind and enter sleep at a deeper level; allowing you to peacefully drift off into a rejuvenating sleep that will give you the rest necessary to wake up the next day with joy in your heart and a spring in your step.

Maximum Enjoyment Every Moment

• • • •

MANIFESTING MIRACLES

Make The Most Of Every Moment With The Ten Inner Teachings

THE TEN INNER TEACHINGS for enlightened living and becoming a magnet for modern-day miracles are:

1. OUTER REFLECTS INNER – *You get what you project, so clean up your self-image for enhanced success.*

2. HIGHLIGHT HIGHEST HOPE – *Know that your heart's greatest desire is an inner experience to save time and effort looking for it in the wrong places.*

3. BE HERE NOW – *The universe exists and operates now. Being present aligns your attention with the point of power when all creation occurs.*

4. REST IN BEING – *Know that You are not your life circumstances. Be aware of your Being during your day to be present, peaceful and powerful.*

5.   LIVE IN LOVE – *Discover that you are one with the most powerful positive force on the planet.*

6.   RESISTANCE IS FUTILE – *To resist life is to resist miracles. Everything happens to help you.*

7.   COMPROMISE CORRODES – *Resolve the conflict between your head and your heart to be congruent in your intentions and actions.*

8.   PRIORITIZE PRAISE – *The antidote to problems and the key to abundance is choosing to praise instead of criticize.*

9.   POSITIVE FOCUS HAS POWER – *You are already getting what you focus on, so you may as well focus on what you want.*

10. LET GO TO LET GROW – *There is a difference between desire and desperation. By being present you are fulfilled and don't need the future to fulfil you.*

By applying these Ten Inner Teachings you can embrace the new, evolve beyond perceiving life events as problems and attract miracles. The end result: maximum enjoyment of every moment!

Embracing the New

Slipping into autopilot as you go from one day to the next can make you numb to true peace, love and joy. If you don't notice all that you are and all that you have, it's hard to appreciate it. If you don't appreciate it, how are you going to really enjoy it? Imagine what you might be missing. Every moment of every day is precious. If you're on autopilot, you risk wasting your gift of life.

Embracing the new is about waking up, tuning in and noticing, appreciating and enjoying all that is already present in THIS MOMENT of your life.

New Beginnings is about focusing on the now rather than focusing on what has or hasn't happened in the past, what might or might not happen in the future, or what needs to be fixed, changed or improved for things to be better.

When you are embracing the new you are fresh and innocent. There is no time to dwell on the past, complain about the present or wish for more in the future. When you are embracing the new, fully in the now, there is no reason to not be happy. You rest within the serenity and splendour of your gift of life. Knowing you are already complete, right now. Aware that nothing in the past is worthwhile thinking about and nothing in the future could be any better than what you are *being*, right now. You are fully present and ready to receive miracles.

Letting Go of Problems

Focusing on things being problems is the quickest way to slow miracles from entering your life.

Choice is the cornerstone of experiencing a problem-free, miraculous life. You can habitually react and judge things to be problems, or you can choose to respond to events with the intent of raising your conscious awareness. By embracing life, you become more evolved, purposeful and present.

Everything that happens during your lifetime is an opportunity for you to evolve. So why cause yourself unnecessary pain by making things into problems?

Whenever you label things as problems, you tend to resist what is. Resistance causes unnecessary stress and limits your joy. When you accept and work through things, you stop creating pain and instead provide yourself with opportunities to live authentically, intuitively, creatively and joyfully.

Evolution relies on things happening in your life that can help you to be things you've never been, know things you've never known and do things you've never done. Therefore, the more unknown or challenging things are, the better, because when you embrace them, you can accelerate your evolution. *New Beginnings* is about letting go of things being problems – for ever!

Manifesting Miracles

Embracing the new and letting go of problems enables you to enjoy your heart's greatest desire (which is an *inner* experience), have nothing to prove (as you live in Love) and recognize that life is unfolding in perfection. As a result, the need to try to improve things, do things and achieve things diminishes. Nevertheless, just because you no longer feel the need to fix life, goals are still valuable. They help you to explore, evolve, play fully in the world and enjoy 200% of life.

Focus less on improving, doing and achieving.
Focus more on loving, being and attracting.

Attract what you want with the power of positive focus, uplifting emotions, presence, praise and non-attachment and by harnessing the power of Om. When manifesting miracles in this way, you take action in the moment, notice how things change and then choose new actions in the next moment. There is no stress or sacrifice because resting in the presence of your own Being is so fulfilling. You don't need the future to fulfil you when you are fully in the here and now. Rather, you experience the perfection and peace that you *already* are and play in the world from a place of joy and service.

New Beginnings is about harnessing the power of the universe, letting go of struggle and becoming a magnet to miracles!

The Kingdom of Heaven is Within
Living with a deep sense of peace, love and joy is the natural by-product of applying the Ten Inner Teachings shared within this book. My advice: choose the ones that resonate with you, be one-pointed in mastering them and a genuine new beginning will be your reward. In doing so it is my hope that you will stop trying to be different, appreciate how perfectly you are being life and directly experience the indescribable beauty of your divine presence.

> *Naturally, you will wake up to the timeless truth that heaven is not a place you get to, but the place that you've been the entire time.*

Let this moment be a new beginning.

Living The Teachings

· · · ·

NEW BEGINNINGS TOOLKIT

42 Tools For Applying The Ten Teachings
To Your Life

WITHIN THIS APPENDIX YOU WILL FIND A RANGE OF TOOLS FOR AP-PLYING THE TEN INNER TEACHINGS TO YOUR LIFE. Each tool has a brief introduction explaining the purpose and benefits, along with instructions. You may want to answer the questions in a separate journal so you can refer to these tools in the future.

TOOL NO. 1 **Your Self-Image**
Knowing you are worthy includes cleaning up your self-image. Use this Tool to become more aware about your current self-image and begin to think about ways to improve it.

What words would you use to describe yourself?

_____

_____

What words would you use to describe the type of life you live?

_____

_____

TOOL NO. 2 **Sources of Self-Speak**

This Tool helps you to see the sources of your self-speak. By exploring where the opinions of the voice in your head came from, you can stop taking your thoughts so seriously. They are simply programs in your mind based upon past conditioning. They don't have to impact your life now! By being more conscious, you can choose to ignore the inner critic and go for what you want, knowing that you are worthy.

Two things my **parents** said about me:

_____

_____

Two things my **teachers** said about me:

_____

_____

Two things my **partners** said about me:

_____

_____

Two things my **friends** have said about me:

_____

_____

Two things **others** have said about me:

_____

_____

TOOL NO. 3 **My Achievements**

You have been achieving great things all your life. This Tool illustrates your natural ability to achieve – so that you start to appreciate how good you actually are. You've done it before and you can do it again! As you think about your earliest and biggest achievements, consider the skills and qualities you used to accomplish these things and the positive consequences.

EXAMPLE OF EARLIEST MEMORY	
Earliest Achievement	Learning to ride bike when I was four years old
Skills/Qualities used	Balance, determination, teamwork

EXAMPLE OF EARLIEST MEMORY cont.	
Positive Consequences	Cycled to work for years and cycled around New Zealand for charity

MY EARLIEST ACHIEVEMENTS	
Earliest Achievement	
Skills/Qualities used	
Positive Consequences	

MY BIGGEST ACHIEVEMENTS	
Biggest Achievement	
Skills/Qualities used	
Positive Consequences	

TOOL NO.4 Personal Power Statement

Clean up your self-image with your very own Personal Power Statement. This Tool helps you to create a powerful affirmation that you can think often to train your brain to be more positive.

Creating Your Personal Power Statement

1. Circle the adjectives, nouns and verbs that resonate with you and add your own.
2. Choose a maximum of three words/statements from each list.
3. Put them together in the following sentence: "I am a (adjectives) (nouns) who (verbs)!"
4. Say your Personal Power Statement with conviction every day at least ten times.
5. Example: *"I am an incredible passionate leader and winner who inspires others, steps up and makes a difference."*

Adjectives

Incredible, Passionate, Outstanding, Beautiful, Brave, Powerful, Dynamic, Joyful, Generous, Amazing, Excited, Energetic, Sensational, Explosive, Sublime, Gorgeous, Strong, Decisive, Breathtaking, Unforgettable, Legendary, Unstoppable, Curious, Fabulous, Warm, Magnificent, Unique, Special, Awesome, Sexy, Loving, Funny, Interesting, Extraordinary, Giving, Adventurous, Compassionate, Creative, Energized, Stunning, Resourceful, Magical, Inspiring, Exotic, Wealthy, Happy, Honest, Genuine, Kind, Patient, Fulfilled, Balanced, Superb, Respectful, Alive, Enlightened, Helpful, Wise, Definite, Content ...

Nouns

Leader, Winner, Helper, Listener, Teacher, Coach, Guider, Lover, Friend, Role Model, Artist, Achiever, Entertainer, Trainer, Soulmate, Maker of Dreams, Champion, The One, Team Player, Mother, Father, Son, Daughter, Brother, Sister, Angel, Millionaire, Fire-walker, Dude, Natural, Gift, Icon, Philosopher, Hero, Spirit, Public Speaker...

Verbs

Inspires Others, Steps Up, Makes a Difference, Walks-the-Talk, Rocks, Motivates Others, Loves Unconditionally, Accepts Others, Gets Results, Sets New Standards, Shines so that Others Shine, Listens, Loves Life, Laughs, Succeeds, Feels Good by Helping Others to Feel Good...

My personal Power Statement is:

_____

_____

_____

TOP TIP

Write your Personal Power Statement on some pieces of paper and put them in locations around your home that you see often, for example a mirror and your fridge.

TOOL NO.5 Valuable Life

Live a life in accordance with your values. This Tool helps you consider how you would like your life to be in light of your values. Decide whether you want to use this Tool to focus on your life in general or on specific areas of your life. Then list the appropriate personal values in your journal and prioritize them, with 1 being the most important value. Write your values list below:

1. _____

2. _____

3. _____

4. _____

5. _____

6. _____

7. _____

8. _____

9. _____

10. _____

Then use that list to write a description of how you would like your life to be in the future, ensuring that you are fulfilling all of your most important values in your description.

Describe how you would like your life to be:

_____

_____

_____

_____

TOOL NO. 6 **Valuable Hints**
**Use these hints to help you determine your general life and con-
text-specific values.**

HINT NO. 1
Imagine an inspirational person and list their values.

1.   Create an imaginary person in your head, who possesses all
     the characteristics of someone you would admire and find
     inspirational.
2.   What would they believe? How would they act? How
     would they see the world? How would they interact with
     others? What would they value as important?
3.   Get an image or sense of this inspirational person in your
     mind's eye now. Write down the values this amazing person
     would have until you reach twenty or thirty values.
4.   Obviously, your list of values will not belong to your
     imaginary person; they are actually the values of another
     incredibly amazing person – YOU!

HINT NO. 2
Identify special, peak moments when life was especially reward-ing or poignant.

1. What was happening, who was present and what was going on?
2. What were the values that were being honoured in that moment?
3. Be aware of the energy hit when you become aware of the value.

HINT NO. 3
Identify times when you were angry, frustrated, or upset.

1. Name the feelings and circumstances around the upset at the time.
2. Flip it over and look for the opposite of these feelings that you experienced.
3. The key here is to be aware that every upset or moment of distress is likely to signal that one or more of your values were being suppressed/challenged.

HINT NO. 4
Identify what you must have in life.

1. Beyond the physical requirements of food, shelter and community, what must you have in your life in order to feel good (be fulfilled)?
2. What are the values you absolutely must honour – or part of you dies?

HINT NO. 5

Identify times when you may have taken certain values to the extreme.

1. What is it that people say about you?
2. What do you say about yourself?

TOOL NO. 7 **Personal Profile**

Get a clear overview of your current life situation. This Personal Profile consists of a series of ten questions designed to gather information about how you think your life is today. It is worth taking your time to answer the questions thoroughly as they will provide a strong foundation of clarity that will help you to move forward. Some questions may be more relevant to you than others. Answer just the questions that are most relevant to you.

Below is the list of Personal Profile Questions:

1. Describe your life at the moment.
2. What three things do you love about your life?
3. What three things do you hate about your life?
4. Describe three of your happiest life memories.
5. List the things that are important to you in your life.
6. If you already have goals, please list them.
7. What are you putting up with in your life?
8. What stops you from doing the things you want in your life?
9. What would you like your epitaph to say?
10. On a blank piece of paper, draw a picture that best illustrates your life at the moment. You are not being tested on your ability to draw. Try to avoid thinking about it too

much. Just start drawing and see what happens – and have fun! Once finished, ask yourself what your picture is telling you about your life.

TOOL NO. 8 101 Life Clarity Questions

The following 101 questions are designed to help you get clarity about your life. Read through the questions and stop to answer the ones that are most relevant to you. There is space at the end of the 101 questions for you to record your ten most important and relevant questions. The ten questions you choose will tell you a great deal about what areas of your life you may like to focus your attention and efforts on.

The 101 Life Clarity Questions are listed below under the ten life-area headings:

Love and Romance with Partner

1. Do you have a partner at the moment?
2. Do you want a partner at the moment?
3. How do you know you are loved by someone else – Is it necessary for you to be taken places and bought things or to be looked at with that special look? Or that you hear that special tone of voice or those special words, or, is it necessary that you are touched in a certain way or a certain place?
4. Does your partner show love towards you in ways you desire?
5. How often do you tell your partner that you love them?
6. How do you show affection towards your partner?
7. How would you rate your love life?
8. How intimate and passionate are you with each other when making love?

9. Do you trust your partner?
10. Do you talk openly with each other?
11. Do you laugh often and have fun together?
12. Does your partner love and appreciate you for who you are without trying to change you?
13. Are you energized or drained by your relationship with your partner?
14. Are you open with yourself and your friends and family about your sexual orientation?

Relationships with Friends and Family

15. Have you told your parents that you love them within the last four weeks?
16. How well do you get along with your siblings?
17. Have you let go of the relationships that drag you down or damage you?
18. Do you gossip or talk about others?
19. Do you have a circle of friends who appreciate you for who you are, more than just what you do for them?
20. Are you fully caught up with letters, emails and calls?
21. Have you fully forgiven those people who have hurt you, intentionally or not?
22. How often do you see your family and friends?
23. How would you rate the quality of your time together?
24. Would you say you were "close" to your friends and family?
25. Do you enjoy open, truthful and caring communications?
26. Do you feel that you could seek support from your family and friends if required?
27. Are you energized or drained by your relationships with your family and friends?

28. Do you spend time with people who don't try to change you, but simply love you for who you are?

Health and Vitality

29. How would you rate your energy levels?
30. How would you rate your general health?
31. Do you have any persistent health problems?
32. Do you drink the recommended amounts of spring water?
33. How would you rate your body's nutrition?
34. Do you walk or exercise at least three times per week?
35. How often do you use caffeine (chocolate, coffee, colas, tea) in a week?
36. How much sugar do you consume daily?
37. How much television do you watch daily?
38. How often do you drink alcohol and when you do, in what quantities?
39. Do you smoke? If yes, how many cigarettes do you smoke a week?
40. How healthy are your teeth and gums?
41. Have you had a complete physical examination in the last three years?
42. Is your weight within or near your ideal range?
43. How well do you hear?
44. Do you have any physical or emotional problems or conditions and are you fully taking care of them all?

Career and Work

45. Are you in a career that is or will soon be financially and personally rewarding?

46. How would you rate your day-to-day work?
47. How would you rate your career prospects?
48. Do you find your work stressful?
49. Do you work your preferred number of hours each week?
50. Are you happy with the amount of work you are required to carry out in your day-to-day work?
51. Do you find your work meaningful and fulfilling?
52. Are your personal values aligned with the values of your job/organization?
53. How would you rate your colleague/client/customer relationships?
54. What skills, knowledge and/or characteristics are you developing in order to carry out your work more efficiently/effectively?
55. Are you rewarded in a manner that is appropriate for the effort and responsibility of your position?

Wealth and Access to Resources

56. Do you feel that you live a life of abundance or a life of scarcity?
57. How much money do you have – current, savings, investments etc.?
58. If you cashed out of your home and/or business tomorrow, how much cash could you raise?
59. What do you own?
60. Who do you know? Consider the people you work with; people you work for; people who work for you; family, friends, neighbours, people you went to school with; people you used to work for; customers/clients etc. Who else? Who do they know? What do they own?

61. What stuff of other people's do you have access to?

Living and Working Environment

62. What is your physical living environment like?
63. Where do you live?
64. How would you rate your place of residence?
65. How would you rate the safety of your street/city/country?
66. How would you rate the cleanliness of your streets/city/country?
67. What is your physical working environment like?
68. How would you rate your place of work?
69. How would you rate your place of education?
70. How would you rate the places you socialize?

Fun and Recreation

71. How much fun do you have in your day-to-day life?
72. Are you as fun as you would like to be?
73. Do you know how to have fun?
74. Do you work and socialize with fun people?
75. Do you carry out fun activities in your personal life?
76. Do you have hobbies that you enjoy?
77. What groups are you a member of?
78. Do you take holidays and if so, where do you go?
79. Do you have something to look forward to most days?
80. Do you know how to relax?
81. What do you do to relax?
82. Would you like to relax more often than you do?

Personal Development and Growth

83. Do you feel that you are developing as a person?
84. What do you do in order to develop and grow?
85. What do you read, watch and listen to in order to develop your self?
86. What seminars, workshops, exhibitions and/or conferences do you attend?
87. What key skills and abilities are you developing at present?

Contribution to Others

88. How do you use your unique abilities, outside of your work, to improve other people's lives?
89. Do you search out ways to contribute to others?
90. Do you give to charity?
91. Do you give your personal resources (skills, time, money etc.) to help others?
92. How often do you give of your personal resources?
93. Do you give as much and as often as you could?
94. If you gave more would you feel more fulfilled?

Spirituality

95. What does the term spirituality mean to you?
96. Is your spirituality at the level you desire?
97. Do you meditate, and if so, do you meditate as often as you would like?
98. Do you live your life in accordance to the attitudes and beliefs that reflect spirituality?
99. How forgiving and accepting are you?

100. Are you aware of other types of spiritual practices?
101. How at peace are you with yourself and your life?

My Top Ten Most Important Questions:

1. _____

2. _____

3. _____

4. _____

5. _____

6. _____

7. _____

8. _____

9. _____

10. _____

TOOL NO. 9 Lifetime Focus

Your life is precious. This Tool helps you to gain clarity on how you would ultimately love your life to be.

Your Age Now ☐

Your Age in Five Years ☐

What five things would you love to achieve within the next five years?

1. _____

2. _____

3. _____

4. _____

5. _____

If you could achieve anything during your lifetime, how would the following aspects of your life be?

Physical _____

_____

_____

Relationships

_____

_____

Career

_____

_____

Financial

_____

_____

HEART'S HIGHEST HOPE: What do you want more than anything else and why?

_____

_____

_____

_____

_____

TOOL NO. 10 **Love Hate Review**

Live a life you love. List all the things in life that you love and hate. Be specific. Consider relationships, career, living and working environment, hobbies and so on. Look for patterns and themes.

I Love

_____

_____

_____

_____

I Hate

_____

_____

_____

_____

Sometimes it is easier to think about what you do NOT want than what you want. You can often discover what you want by considering the things you hate and then flipping them. For instance, if you hate being "stuck in an office" then you may find that you love the "freedom from being outdoors around nature and in fresh air".

TOOL NO.11 Feelgood Times

Discover more about the things you enjoy in life. Think of a specific time when you felt good and answer the questions below. Look for patterns, themes and insights.

What were you doing?	
Where were you doing it?	
How were you doing it?	
What were you feeling?	
Why were you feeling that way?	
What else is relevant?	

TOOL NO.12 Impact Goals

Your time is precious. It is wise to use it to improve things that have the greatest impact on your happiness.

Improving what two relationships would have the greatest impact upon your life?	
Delegating what two things would have the greatest impact upon your life?	
Cleaning up what two messes would have the greatest impact upon your life?	
Developing what two capabilities would have the greatest impact upon your life?	
Establishing what two habits would have the greatest impact upon your life?	

Now complete the "Scoring Goals" Tool on the next page to ensure that the above goals will have a positive impact upon your entire life.

TOOL NO.13 Scoring Goals

How will achieving your desired outcome improve each area of your life? Tick the life area(s) that achieving your outcome will improve (in the "Outcome Scoring" column). Add up the ticks to get a total score out of 10. Give reasons as to why you ticked each area as you did. The purpose of this Tool is to help you to focus your time and effort upon the outcomes that improve your life the most.

STATE GOAL		
	Outcome Scoring	Reason for Scoring
Love & Romance		
Family & Friends		
Health & Vitality		
Career & Work		
Money & Wealth		
Environment		
Fun & Recreation		
Personal Growth		
Contribution		
Spirituality		
TOTAL SCORING		

Did your outcome score highly enough? If no, go back and explore what you REALLY want. If yes, turn to the "Creating M.E.A.N.T. T.O. B.E. Outcomes" Tool to start manifesting miracles!

TOOL NO.14 Your Dream Team

Surround yourself with a dream team who are nurturing. Write the names of the people in your life who are on your team – the people who accept, challenge, support and love you exactly as you are now. These people are your Dream Team because they want you to go for your dream life. Write the names of everyone else in your life in the Other People category. You can continue to love the "Other People" exactly as they are, while surrounding yourself more closely with your Dream Team.

TOOL NO. 15 **About M.E.A.N.T. T.O. B.E. Goals**

Have the universe on your side when accomplishing your goals.
To do this, you can word them in such a way that makes them seem "meant to be". M.E.A.N.T. T.O. B.E. is an acronym that stands for:

M E A N T

| Meaningful Mission | Energising & Exciting | Achievement Ambitious | Now Present | Timings Realistic |

T O B E

| Towards Dreams | Owned & Optimistic | Beliefs Honoured | Ethical & Universal |

MEANINGFUL MISSION: The outcome has a strong "why".

ENERGIZING & EXCITING: The outcome energizes you.

ACHIEVABLE & AMBITIOUS: The outcome challenges you.

NOW PRESENT: The outcome is stated in the present tense.

TIMINGS REALISTIC: The outcome has a completion date.

TOWARDS DREAMS: The outcome helps you achieve life goals.

OWNED & OPTIMISTIC: The outcome is owned and positive.

BELIEFS HONOURED: The outcome is congruent with your personal beliefs.

ETHICAL & UNIVERSAL: The outcome does no harm to anyone and provides the opportunity for you to benefit yourself & all of humanity.

TOOL NO. 16 Manifesting M.E.A.N.T. T.O. B.E. Goals

Make the manifestation of your dreams feel inevitable. The best way to use this Tool is to have someone ask you the questions and for you to allow your unconscious mind to answer. To do this, sit quietly and without replying verbally; just nod your head when you get a sense that the question has been answered by your unconscious mind (so your assistant knows when to ask the next question). You may find by the end of the questions that your goal feels closer, brighter, more achievable and inevitable!

1. What specifically do you want?
2. Where are you now?
3. For what purpose do you want this?
4. What will you see, hear and feel when you have it?
5. How will you know when you have it?
6. What will this outcome get for you?
7. What will this outcome allow you to do?
8. Who is achieving the outcome dependent upon?
9. Where do you want it?
10. When do you want it?
11. How do you want it?
12. With whom do you want it?
13. What beliefs do you have now that will help you?
14. What beliefs do you need to have now to have it?
15. What do you have now, and what do you need to get your outcome?
16. Have you ever had or done this before?
17. Do you know anyone who has?
18. What will you lose if you have it?
19. What will you gain if you have it?
20. How will achieving this outcome improve the world?

TOOL NO. 17 **Peace Exists Now**

Notice what you are focusing on whenever you feel bad. You might find that in order for you to feel negative emotions, you need to focus on a past memory or future possibility. By contrast, inner peace, love, joy and/or contentment are experienced when you are focused on the present moment.

Think of a time when you felt anger. Where was your focus?	
Think of a time when you felt sad. Where was your focus?	
Think of a time when you felt guilt. Where was your focus?	
Think of a time when you felt anxiety. Where was your focus?	
Think of a time when you felt contentment. Where was your focus?	

TOOL NO.18 Stop Watch

One way to begin to notice the moment more is to tune in to your senses. This Tool can give you guidance on how to stop and watch the moment via your senses.

SEE

Notice what you can see.
Only look, without labelling. Look at the colours. Look at the shapes. Look at the textures. Notice the light. Look at the distance between objects. Be aware of the space. Focus on individual objects, noticing things about them you may have previously missed. Now expand your vision out into the periphery of what you can see. See all that is to the left of you and to the right of you. Now see all that is above and below your eye level.

FEEL

Notice what you feel.
Now notice all that you are touching. Notice your clothes, the ground and the chair you may be sitting on. Feel the air dancing all around you, all so lovingly touching every part of you. Feel the temperature. The air flowing in and out of you. How it feels to just breathe. Feel your life inside and around you. Just feel.

HEAR

Now listen to the sounds.
Tune in. Avoid labelling or judging. Just listen. Allow yourself to notice a sound that you had not heard until now. Now listen to the silence that allows the sounds. And the sound that allows the silence. Notice all that you can taste and smell. Embrace your senses.

TOOL NO.19 **Magic in the Mundane**

Even mundane tasks can become magical if you are present. This Tool provides guidance on how to do this.

DAILY COMMUTE
When travelling... to places either by foot, car, bus, plane or train, stay present. Focus on the journey, not the destination. Aim to fully experience every step. There is incredible beauty, love and humour all around. Notice it.
DAILY TASKS
When cleaning... yourself, your house, your car and even your dishes! Be attentive to your senses. See how the light reflects. Tune in to all the sounds along with the silence that allows all the sounds. Be aware of how things feel in your hands.
DAILY CHATS!
When talking... to friends, family, colleagues, neighbours and others, aim to be fully present in every aspect of the experience; what you can hear, see and feel. Listen attentively to the end of the other person's sentences and then allow a moment of complete silence before responding. Give every single person you meet your fullest attention, irrespective of "what's in it for you", or how "important" you may have judged the person to be.
DAILY ANYTHING!
When... being or doing anything! With anything you do every day, have the intention to stay aware of the magnificent moment happening.

TOOL NO.20 **3C Vision**

Use your eyes for a positive change. Use this Tool to be present, clear your mind and feel calm, confident and content.

INSTRUCTIONS:

1. Pick a spot on the wall to look at, ideally above eye level, so that as you look at it, it feels as though your vision is bumping up against your eyebrows.
2. As you stare at the spot on the wall, effortlessly let your mind go loose and focus all of your attention on the spot. At this point you may find yourself wanting to take a deep breath in and out. Let yourself do so.
3. Notice that almost instantly, your vision will begin to spread out. You will begin to see more in the peripheral than in the central part of your vision.
4. Now, pay more attention to the peripheral part of your vision than to the central part of your vision. Keep looking ahead whilst also noticing colours, shadows and shapes in your periphery. Notice what you see on the left and right, above and below.
5. Notice how it feels and if your mind is more still.

With a little practice you will be able to use 3C Vision as you go about your day – when reading, out walking, chatting with people, pretty much any time you want to feel calm, confident and content.

TOOL NO. 21 **Who You Think You Are**

You are not what you think. Use this Tool to discover the difference between you and your life circumstances. Hint: You are not your job title, marital status etc.

Imagine you are at a party and someone asks you the question: *"So who are you?"* How would you answer?

Notice the difference between who you think you are and what you do.

TOP TIP

Who You Are is permanent, unchanging and is not what you do within your external life circumstances. You are the conscious awareness that is aware of whatever you are doing in any given moment.

TOOL NO. 22 Love Levels

Evaluate how loving you are towards yourself and other people.
This is an awareness-raising exercise, so use what you discover to
be gentle towards yourself and your life and make loving changes if
and where required.

LOVING YOURSELF
On a scale of 1–10, how much would you say you love and accept yourself exactly as you are today?
1   2   3   4   5   6   7   8   9   10   +MORE
WHAT DO YOU NOT LOVE AND ACCEPT ABOUT YOURSELF?

LOVING LIFE
On a scale of 1–10, how much would you say you love and accept your life for what it is today?
1   2   3   4   5   6   7   8   9   10   +MORE
WHAT DO YOU NOT LOVE AND ACCEPT ABOUT YOUR LIFE?

Notice your reasons for NOT loving yourself, other people and
your life unconditionally. Be willing to let them go to be free to
love fully.

TOOL NO. 23 The Judgement Game

Judgement puts your life in a box. Learning to judge less requires you to see The Judgement Game that your mind continuously engages in. When the mind judges life it puts what happens into one or more of the six boxes below. For example, if you have a problem with a person, then you might put them in the "WRONG" or "BAD" box.

STEP ONE: Put a person or situation that you are currently judging into one or more of the following boxes:

Good	Bad
Right	Wrong
Better	Worse

STEP TWO: Now put what you are judging in this box:

It Just Is

STEP THREE: Notice how it feels to let things be. Notice what you are judging and resisting as bad, wrong or worse and choose to be free by letting life be.

TOOL NO.24 **Getting Unstuck**

Feeling stuck with a problem? Establish what you have in your resource bank with this Tool. Use what you discover to put your ideas into action: make some calls, spend some money, use your stuff and prepare to be amazed!

WHAT IS THE PROBLEM?	
You The qualities, skills, gifts and talents you bring to the world, including: Kindness, humour and creativity ...	
Other People Every person knows an average of 250 people. Who do you know that could help you? Who do they know?	
Money How much money do you have – current, savings, investments etc?	
Other Stuff What do you own? What stuff of other people's do you have access to?	
What Steps Can You Take To Get Unstuck?	

TOOL NO.25 Situation Reframe

Change how you think about things and the things you think about change. By thinking about a situation from a more positive and productive perspective, you can see things you hadn't seen before.

Describe a problematic situation that requires your creativity.

If you had magical powers and could do anything you wanted, what would you do?

What advice would you give someone else in a similar situation to you?

What will be important about this situation one year from now?

TOOL NO. 26 **Quantum Thinking**

Quantum Thinking is an immensely powerful way of helping you to think "outside the box". It helps you to think beyond your usual way of thinking to find creative solutions to problematic situations. When faced with a problem, use the four different ways of structuring questions. The goal: To come up with creative solutions that you would not normally consider within the usual thinking parameters of your mind. Your mind may initially say that you don't know the answer. Ignore this thought. Rest and allow your inner knowing to arise.

+ +

Perception of FUTURE
What will happen if you don't do/get it?

Perception of PROBLEM
What is the problem?

Perception of LEARNING
What is it you know you know?

- +

Perception of FUTURE
What won't happen if you do/get it?

Perception of PROBLEM
What is the problem not?

Perception of LEARNING
What is it you don't know you know?

+ -

Perception of FUTURE
What will happen if you don't do/get it?

Perception of PROBLEM
What do you need to know for this to be a problem?

Perception of LEARNING
What is it you know you don't know?

- -

Perception of FUTURE
What won't happen if you don't do/get it?

Perception of PROBLEM
What do you need to not know for this to be a problem?

Perception of LEARNING
What is it you don't know you don't know?

EXAMPLE **Explore Solutions with Quantum Thinking:**
What is the problem?
I'm upset because my dad shouted at me when I was a child.
What is the problem not?
The problem is not happening any more. (Hmmm, I had not considered this before!)
What do you need to know for this to be a problem?
I need to know that Dad did it because he hated me (Hmmm, this doesn't feel true as I think about it now as an adult.)
What do you need to not know for this to be a problem?
I need to not know that my dad loves me. (I had never considered

this before because I was focused on being shouted at. I'm feeling bet-
ter about the childhood event now as I'm able to focus more on how
my dad loves me.)

TOOL NO. 27 **Letting Go**

Let go of your problem, for good. Only use this process if you are
willing to let go of the problem now. It can help you to have a shift
in perspective so you see beyond it being a problem and embrace
the opportunity to raise your consciousness and enhance your evolution.

1. Do you have a problem that you would like to let go of?
2. How have you benefited from allowing it to be a problem
    up until now?
3. How could you benefit from stopping it from being a
    problem now?
4. What had you, up until now, been resisting about the situa-
    tion?
5. What could you learn so that this situation stops being a
    problem and, instead, helps your personal evolution?
6. What happens within you if you actively choose to make
    your peace more important than this problem?

Imagine any remaining resistance completely leaving you now
and being replaced with pure acceptance. Remember, it isn't good
or bad, right or wrong, better or worse. It just is. Take a few deep
breaths as you notice, appreciate and enjoy how differently you feel
towards the situation which you previously thought and felt was a
problem.

TOOL NO.28 Hindsight Helps

With the passage of time we can often see how positive past problems actually were. Use this Tool to consider how past events that you thought were a problem at the time may have actually had a positive impact upon your life.

Examples to consider include relationship break-ups, job losses and other events that you thought were problems.

PAST PROBLEM ...	HOW IT HELPED ME ...

TOOL NO.29 **Freedom from Fear**

Make fear your friend. This Tool can help you to stop fear from stopping you from taking action. By no longer resisting the feelings of fear, while clearing the hidden benefits of holding on to the fear, you can "befriend the fear" and use it to help you to take empowered action.

What's been stopping you from taking action? Is it the fear of not being good enough, not being loved, not getting what you want or not keeping what you've got? Or a combination of the above? Be honest.

How have you been benefiting from allowing the fear to stop you until now? What is it that you are doing that you enjoying doing but won't be able to do if the fear disappears?

What do you need to know in order to let the fear go? The emotion exists for a beneficial reason. What do you need to know or learn, the knowing or learning of which will make the fear disappear?

What happens if you stop resisting the feeling? Where is the feeling of fear in your body? What happens to it if you say "BRING IT ON" to the feeling?

TOOL NO. 30 Hidden Benefits

You are less likely to let go of a problem if you are benefiting from keeping it. This Tool can help you to become aware of how you might be benefiting from keeping a problem.

What is the problem?

If you were to be **honest** with yourself, how might you be benefiting from keeping this problem?

What are you **not doing** because you have this problem?

What is it you are doing, which you **enjoy** doing but won't be able to do if you no longer have this problem?

What is the problem preventing you from doing, which you will **have to do** if you no longer have this problem?

TOOL NO.31 Observing Obligations

Every obligation is closely followed by a "should". If you act because you feel you "should" then there can be an inner resistance that is detrimental to both your peace and your prosperity. FOR EXAMPLE: Resisting looking after an ill relative. If you find that you are acting out of obligation, it doesn't mean you have to stop what you are doing. The key is to acknowledge that it is YOUR CHOICE to be it, do it or have it. When you then continue in the knowledge that it is YOUR CHOICE, you stop being a victim and do it because you want it.

What are you **DOING** because you think you should?	
What do you **HAVE** because you think you should?	
What are you **BEING** because you think you should?	

No Obligation = No Resistance = No Negative Emotions = No Problem

TOOL NO. 32 Choosing Praise

Praise is the antidote to experiencing life as a problem. This Tool helps you to find the things in your life that you are currently criticizing and think about ways of praising them instead. The result is: a miraculous and immediate improvement in the way you feel – irrespective of whether the external things change or not.

What Things Are You Currently Criticizing In Your Life?	What Can You Praise And Appreciate About These Things?

TOOL NO.33 Loving Intent

You will attract your intentions. It is vitally important that you get clear on your underlying intentions for being, doing or having the things you want. Use this Tool to ensure that your intent is positive and loving. Awareness is key with this exercise. I've discovered that by highlighting any negative intentions it is possible to set the inner intention to go for what you want with love.

What Do You Want?	Why Do You Want It?

TOOL NO. 34 About Creating States

All emotions reside within you. Any emotional state you desire exists within you now. Cultivating positive emotions helps you to become a magnet for miracles. Creating any state you want requires the following three ingredients:

YOUR PHYSIOLOGY

The most powerful way to change your state is to use your physiology. You can adapt your breathing (deep and balanced), posturing (chest out, shoulders back), solid stance, eye positioning (looking up) and body movements (expressive, animated etc) in order to change your emotional state.

YOUR FOCUS

You feel what you focus on i.e. where you direct your attention. So focus on what you want (rather than on what you don't want!). For example, instead of focusing on not being confident, focus on courage.

YOUR SELF-SPEAK

The things you say to yourself and how you say them influences how you feel. You can use the "Personal Power Statement" on pages 118–119 to help you think positively about yourself.

TOOL NO.35 **Creating States**

Use this Tool to guide you when creating states:

YOUR PHYSIOLOGY How could you use your body to create the desired state? Examples: Raise chest, big smile, breathe deeply etc	
YOUR FOCUS What could you focus on to create the desired state? Remember – focus on what you want rather than what you don't want	
YOUR SELF-SPEAK What could you say to yourself and how could you say it to yourself to create the desired state? (Also see Personal Power Statement Tool for help.)	

TOOL NO. 36 Gratitude Attitude

I'M GRATEFUL FOR THE FOLLOWING:	
Love & Romance	
Family & Friends	
Health & Vitality	
Career & Work	
Money & Wealth	
Environment	
Fun & Recreation	
Personal Growth	
Contribution	
Spirituality	
Name a person that you are grateful for having in your life.	
How are you going to show this person that you are grateful for them over the next seven days?	

TOOL NO. 37 Acknowledging Attachments

Holding on hurts the hands that hold. Having desires is natural and can lead to you enjoying a wonderful life. Attachment on the other hand is exhausting and can lead to stress, suffering, frustration and fear. Use this Tool to discover the things in your life that you are attached too. Remember, if you think you NEED it to be happy, peaceful or loved, then you are attached to it. By letting go of needing it, you can still be, do or have it, but non-attachment means you get to truly enjoy it without fear.

What do you **NEED** to **be** in order to feel happy, peaceful or loved?	
What do you **NEED** to **do** in order to feel happy, peaceful or loved?	
What do you **NEED** to **have** in order to feel happy, peaceful or loved?	

Remember: attachment makes you a slave to Life's golden carrots. Let go to let good grow!

TOOL NO. 38 **Om Thought Meditation Instructions**

Harness the power of Om to transform your life. Do this meditation 2–3 times every day for ten minutes (or more). Good times of the day are before breakfast, before dinner and before bed. Use the following instructions:

1. HEART'S GREATEST DESIRE

Decide what you want more than anything else. Please make sure it is stated in the positive: for example peace, love, vitality, courage, contentment ...

2. GET COMFORTABLE

Sit on a chair, sofa or even on your bed. Wear loose clothes, support yourself with cushions and wrap yourself in a blanket if there's a chance you could get chilly.

3. GENTLY BE AWARE OF NOW

With your eyes closed, let your attention rest wide as you remain alert. Notice that this moment is happening. Be inwardly aware of the still quiet presence that exists within your Being. This takes no effort, no straining or trying.

4. OCCASIONALLY THINK YOUR OM THOUGHT

Gently think your Om Thought – "Om Love" or "Om Peace" etc – and then let it go. Do not try to hold it in your mind. Just stay alert and watch whatever happens immediately. After a while your mind will become active and you will start thinking. When you notice that you've been thinking, gently rethink your Om Thought. For the rest of your meditation, slowly go between noticing now, thinking your Om Thought, noticing now until you start thinking, rethinking your Om Thought, and so on. Go back and forth, in a very easy and comfortable way.

TOOL NO. 39 **Process for Attracting Goals**

Attract what you want with effortless ease. This simple process opens you up for abundance to flow into your life. I use it for attracting my own goals and also to help my clients attract theirs, often with miraculous results! When using the process, you take action in the moment, notice how things change and then choose new actions in the next moment. There is no stress or sacrifice. As you focus on what you want, appreciate every step of your journey and trust that your desire will manifest in the perfect way at the perfect time.

Be a Magnet for Miracles with this simple process:

1. FOCUS
Focus on your goal with loving intent. Imagine what you will see, hear, feel, smell and taste when it is manifested.

2. IMAGINE
Cup your hands in front of you and imagine gently placing what you want in the palm of your hand.

3. APPRECIATE
For a few moments, appreciate it, now, as if you've already attracted it into your life.

4. BREATHE
Breathe three breaths of life into the image of what you want.

5. MANIFEST
Now, imagine what you want effortlessly rising up and flying into your future to manifest at a time that is most perfect for you.

TOOL NO. 40 Daily Review

Keep on track using this Daily Review. Ask yourself the following questions every morning and night.

MORNING QUESTIONS	
What am I going to do today to move myself towards my goals? Also, what am I going to do to make today one of the best days of my life?	

EVENING QUESTIONS	
What have I done today to move towards my goals? What did I learn? What did I give? How did I share my love with others?	

TOOL NO.41 **Energy Sources**

Meet the universe halfway by enhancing your energy. For the key energy sources, rate from 1–10 (with 10 being high), how well you are currently enhancing your energy.

BREATHE FOR LIFE
Deep Belly Balanced Breathing
1 2 3 4 5 6 7 8 9 10

DRINK FOR LIFE
Spring Water Intake
1 2 3 4 5 6 7 8 9 10

EAT FOR LIFE
Real Food, Not Too Much, Mostly Plants
1 2 3 4 5 6 7 8 9 10

MOVE FOR LIFE
Regular Endorphin-Releasing Exercise
1 2 3 4 5 6 7 8 9 10

REST FOR LIFE
Good Sleeping Patterns
1 2 3 4 5 6 7 8 9 10

TAKE ACTION: What are you going to commit to doing in order to enhance your energy?

TOOL NO. 42 **Balanced Breathing**

Breathing is one of the simplest and most effective ways to enhance energy. Research by the Institute of HeartMath in the US (based on over fifteen years of scientific investigation into stress and the relationship between the heart and brain) has recorded massive benefits from balancing your breathing. They have found that breathing in and out for equal amounts of time almost immediately causes what is referred to as "high heart coherence". Heart coherence refers to the smoothness of the rhythms of your heart. Smooth rhythms are less stressful for the body and can also help you to enhance the energy of your body–mind.

INSTRUCTIONS: Repeatedly breathe in for a count of five or six seconds (whichever is most comfortable), and then breathe out for the same length of time.

TOP TIP

You may find it useful to set aside time in your day to do this. Good times include while having a shower in the morning, when in transit on a bus or train or while meditating.

An oxygenated body is an energized body. Doing this simple exercise will help you get yourself out of a stressed state, enjoy greater wellbeing and has even been scientifically proven to enhance the immune system.

EXPLORING THE BOOK

•••••

New Beginnings Questions

10 Questions For Exploring The Ten Teachings

WITHIN THIS APPENDIX YOU WILL FIND TEN QUESTIONS FOR EX-PLORING THE KEY MESSAGES IN THE BOOK. Read through the questions and consider the ones that most resonate with you. All answers exist within you now. The right question at the right moment can help you to access your inner wisdom. You may want to answer the questions in a journal so you can refer to them in the future.

TOOL NO. 1   New Beginnings Questions

Use these questions to explore some of the key topics:

1. If now is all that is real, what are you waiting for before you embrace it?
2. What conditions may you be attaching to loving yourself, other people and the world?
3. What area(s) of your life are you currently resisting?
4. What are you being, doing and having out of obligation?
5. What are you focusing on? Is it what you want?
6. What do you want the meaning of your life to be?

7. What would you do, and how would you be, if today were going to be one of the best days of your life?
8. How might you be stopping what you want from flowing into your life?
9. How does what you want in this moment differ from what you want in the future?
10. What people, places, events and things could you feel grateful for in this moment?

THE NEW BEGINNING CONTINUES

• • • • •

Next Steps

You're Going To Love What You Can Do Next

CLUB: Join Sandy's online club where you can access videos, audios and articles and special offers.

CLINICS: Experience a private one-to-one Mind Detox and/or Mind Calm consultation with Sandy or find a Mind Detox Practitioner or Mind Calm Coach near you using Sandy's online Practitioner Finder.

COURSES: Learn more advanced forms of meditation with Sandy that are only ever taught in person.

RETREATS: Experience Sandy's unique mind-body-soul approach to health, peace and happiness at one of his residential retreats. Highly recommended!

ACADEMY: Make a positive difference to the lives of others by training with Sandy to become a qualified Mind Detox Method (MDM) Practitioner or Mind Calm Method (MCM) Coach with Sandy's award-winning Academy.

For more info, visit: *www.sandynewbigging.com*

About the Author

SANDY C. NEWBIGGING is the creator of the Mind Detox and Mind Calm methods of therapy and meditation, and author of several books including *Heal the Hidden Cause, Life Detox, Life-Changing Weight Loss* and *Thunk!*. His work has been seen on television worldwide on channels including Discovery Health.

Sandy has clinics in the UK, runs residential retreats internationally and trains Mind Detox practitioners and Mind Calm coaches via his academy. He was recently commended by the Federation of Holistic Therapists as "tutor of the year" and has been described by *Yoga Magazine* as being *"one of the best meditation teachers around"*.

For more information on talks and workshops given by Sandy C. Newbigging or to book him for a speaking event, please use the following contact details:

answers@sandynewbigging.com
www.facebook.com/minddetoxman
www.twitter.com/minddetoxman
www.sandynewbigging.com

Acknowledgements

INFINITE GRATITUDE GOES TO MKI. Your guidance has helped me move from "knowing about" to "directly experiencing" the teachings shared in this book.

Big thanks, as always, goes to the Newbigging clan and to my good friends Bryce Redford, Lee Johnson, Micci Gorrod, Andrew Pepper, Esther Pepper, Calum Murray, Richard Abbot, Stewart Pearce and Sasha Allenby for the love, laughs and learning you bring into my life.

Special thanks goes to David R. Hamilton PhD for contributing the foreword, and big appreciation goes to the team at Findhorn Press, including Sabine Weeke, Jacqui Lewis, Thierry Bogliolo, Carol Shaw and Richard Crookes. Releasing three books in twelve months involves a great deal of work and I appreciate your professionalism and positivity throughout.

Gratitude also goes to the bestselling authors who took the time to read *New Beginnings* and give such encouraging praise, including Ursula James, Timothy Freke, Barefoot Doctor, Suzy Greaves, Joseph Clough, Nick Williams and Shamesh Aladina.

My heartfelt thanks also goes to every person who has attended my talks, clinics, academy courses and retreats. Without your courage to go for what you want this book would not have been possible.

Further Sandy C. Newbigging Titles

Heal the Hidden Cause

In this ground-breaking book, Sandy C. Newbigging shows you how by making peace with your past, chronic stress is reduced, allowing the body to heal. In addition, clearing your self-limiting beliefs helps you to use your mind to achieve brilliant success in business and life.

978-1-84409-614-5

Thunk!

Bridging the gap between serenity and success, this enlightening guide depicts the mind as a tool to be picked up and used as required and then put away when it's no longer needed, allowing for improvements in relationships, creativity, and intuitive-decision making.

978-1-84409-603-9

FINDHORN PRESS

Life-Changing Books

For a complete catalogue,
please contact:

Findhorn Press Ltd
117-121 High Street,
Forres IV36 1AB,
Scotland, UK

t +44 (0)1309 690582
f +44 (0)131 777 2711
e info@findhornpress.com

or consult our catalogue online
(with secure order facility) on
www.findhornpress.com

For information on the Findhorn Foundation:
www.findhorn.org